HOW TO FIGHT BACK

How To
Fight Back

NICKY CRUZ

KINGSWAY PUBLICATIONS
EASTBOURNE

Copyright © Nicky Cruz 1991

First published in the USA by
New Leaf Press, Green Forest, Arkansas

First British edition 1991

Front cover illustration by Vic Mitchell

British Library Cataloguing in Publication Data

Cruz, Nicky
  How to fight back.
  I. Title
  248.4

  ISBN 0-86065-863-5

Printed in Great Britain for
KINGSWAY PUBLICATIONS LTD
1 St Anne's Road, Eastbourne, E. Sussex BN21 3UN by
Richard Clay Ltd, Bungay, Suffolk
Reproduced from the original text by arrangement with
New Leaf Press

A Note of
Explanation

Many of the names of real people and locales in this book have been changed in the interest of privacy and to protect the innocent.

In some instances, similar testimonies have been told as one story — further preserving the anonymity of those involved.

Thanks to former satanist Glen Littel, and other such friends for their candor as they told their incredible, true stories.

I thank them for understanding as my editors and I saw the need to protect them by disguising their circumstances, although they were perfectly willing to stand boldly against the forces of evil, name names, and proclaim the might and power of the Lord who was their strength as they learned ... HOW TO FIGHT BACK!

Contents

I dedicate this book to my youngest daughter, my beloved Elena Mia, who was not yet born at the time I dedicated my book *The Lonely Now* to my other lovely daughters, Alicia, Laura and Nicole. I am so proud of Elena for her diligence in school and for being such an obedient daughter.

I also dedicate this book to my beautiful firstborn grandchild, Isabella Cruz Dow, and to the other grand-children who will follow. Isabella is indeed a crown to her grandfather (Prov. 17:6).

My prayer is for the Lord to pour out His blessings upon my children and grandchildren and protect them from all the evil forces until Jesus returns. Proverbs 14:26: "He who fears the Lord has a secure fortress, and for his children, it will be a refuge."

Acknowledgments

Thanks to my special friends who have contributed greatly to this book:

- To Christian psychologist, Dr. Larry Taylor, a true friend whose insight proved to be a valuable resource;
- To Miss Gretchen Hammond, "a special bookworm" who freely donated her time to proof-read and correct;
- To my son-in-law, Patrick Dow, for being so thorough and supervising all of my scripts, for correcting and editing and for being a student of the English language; and
- Lastly, to my office staff for their faithfulness and hard work.

1
Risking Your Kids

Island Pond is a pretty little town, straight out of an old Currier & Ives print — rural America at its most picturesque. Yet behind the rural façade, is a spine-tingling horror story of spiritual warfare straight out of the best-selling Christian novel *This Present Darkness*.

But *this* tale is true.

It was here recently that forces of evil collided with a faithful, prayerful remnant on their knees. It was here that a diabolical plot more insidious than any novel was thwarted through direct, dramatic intervention by the forces of the Almighty God.

Imagine, if you will, this battle scene:

• One-hundred-twelve weeping Christian youngsters being herded by Vermont State Police onto chartered buses;

• Horrified parents held at gunpoint by helmeted, flak-jacketed police and sneering welfare officials — then dropping to their knees and beseeching our God to halt this terrible seizure of their kids;

• Vermont state officials briefing the assembled international press that these rosy-cheeked, chorus-singing children were actually severely abused and brainwashed by these dangerous, religious fundamentalists — and were being protected by the state from their parents, who were in a dangerous cult that practiced spanking and did not believe in evolution or material possessions!

How could this happen in America, the "Land of the Free, Home of the Brave?" New England is the birthplace of the American Revolution! In adjacent New Hampshire, even car tags proclaim, "Live Free or Die!"

Yet, it was in this picturesque hamlet that troopers and social workers swept in at dawn one Saturday and seized 112 Christian children from their beds — after a secret investigation determined that members of the Community Church in Island Pond spanked their children with lightweight dowel rods purchased at the hardware store.

"These people actively proselyted," the gawking press was told by officials. "Regularly, they took their children on week-long recruitment trips with the admitted intent of bringing in more members to their group."

That's another way of saying they witnessed to others about Jesus — taking their own kids on seven-day jaunts down the popular hiking trails — with tents and backpacks, expecting to win to Jesus some of the thousands of vacationers trekking the scenic New England mountain paths maintained by the National Park Service, the state and nature groups.

And, said officials, these religious nuts were teaching little kids that humanism is a lie, that creationism is a reality and that respecting authority is ordained by God.

For these crimes, the parents deserved to lose their children.

The kids needed to be "rescued" by the state.

I don't tell this story to scare you — but rather to prepare you. The forces that hate us, my friends, are filled with a terrible anger. Their attack is mounting worldwide against us. They hate the truth that we know.

They want Christian children.

But they cannot have them. Our God is not defeated by the mere devices of evil men and rebel angels. You and your children have the tools to fight back — *and win* in the power of the Almighty Creator of the Universe.

The final battle has begun.

But you can (and will) win — if you will only be as faithful as the Christian moms and dads of Island Pond, Vermont.

Some time ago, a group of evangelistic former Jesus People led by Elbert Spriggs came to Island Pond from Chattanooga, Tennessee. The group had been worshipping together for about six years. In their new rural home, they began to worship at their Community Church, which they opened to anyone.

There is no denying that the very conservative local Vermont populace took their arrival with some alarm. These former Tennesseans looked like hippies. Member's dress was reminiscent of the 1970s Jesus movement. The men had beards and ponytails — and wore bib overalls. The women kept their heads covered with kerchiefs and their ankles hidden in "granny" dresses.

Even harder to take was the church's repudiation of materialism and their belief in sharing all they had with one another. But after all, this concept was apparently practiced by the early church in Jerusalem, according to Acts 4:32-35. And such radical concepts as denial of possessions have been practiced by priests, nuns and monks of the Roman Catholic church for several hundred years.

Despite some reports, the Island Pond Community Church was not a classic "commune." Families remained together — with husbands and wives and kids living together in apartments within church-purchased houses and in an old hotel. But the group had a common purse. All purchases were made by elders — usually after much prayer.

The church owns almost no motor vehicles. Instead, members espouse their belief in the wholesomeness of their long evangelistic "walks" throughout New England's scenic vacation trails — such as Jesus took between Galilee and Judea with His apostles.

The more that locals observed the straight-laced group, the more their concern grew about the town being taken over by "religious fanatics." Rumors began to spread in the Island Pond area about church-ordered child switchings — particularly of the little boy who was disciplined for making believe a piece of wood was a truck during a church service.

Church elders such as James Howell defend the group's admittedly disciplined lifestyle. Doctrinally, they say they only accept the Bible as their text. They believe in depending on the Lord for everything.

They teach the need to seek Him in all things.

They wait on Him.

They praise Him in all things.

Satan hates such people.

And so, the Community Church made a lot of enemies.

One local woman freely calls the church a cult and will talk at length with anyone who asks about her disapproval of those who spank their children.

She talks about befriending disgruntled church members and of leading two town meetings which she called. There, rumors flew and denunciations were leveled at church members — such as accusations that the group was secretly aligned with the Moonies or Hare Krishna or some other weird cult.

Strategies were planned to shut down the "commune" by legal means.

The most repeated charges were that the children were not in a state-certified school. Truancy charges were filed by the Essex County State's Attorney, then were thrown out of court. After all, the children were home-schooled together in an informal private school and consistently tested higher than the children attending local public schools.

State welfare department officials then followed up child abuse and spanking allegations. They filed a petition claiming that five youngsters in the church were "in need of supervision" because their parents had spanked them. Those charges were also dropped for lack of evidence.

But state welfare department officials grew vicious when the church refused to allow case workers to begin inspecting the school, the church's nursery, the family apartments — and particularly to interrogate the children without their parents in attendance.

Some months before, several local folks went to visit the local prosecuting attorney and a sympathetic district judge. They cited the frustrations of welfare workers and requested a warrant to search the church's nineteen buildings and seize any evidence — particularly any abused children.

The judge spent four hours reviewing the case. He decided to sign the warrant. Local welfare officials were authorized to organize the raid. They enlisted help from the Vermont attorney general — who had just declared his candidacy for governor.

The local prosecuting attorney got enthusiastic backing from the State Department of Social and Rehabilitation Services, whose welfare workers were furious over being rebuffed in their repeated attempts to inspect the facilities and get the kids alone for questioning about spanking and religious "brain-washing."

At dawn, Island Pond was silent.

At 6:30 a.m., the 300 or so members of the Community Church were still asleep when the clatter of news media helicopters, state-chartered buses, police cars and a convoy of official vehicles broke the morning's stillness. With SWAT-team precision, 90 shotgun-toting troopers and deputized officials in flak jackets charged into the hamlet.

By 6:38 a.m., teams of four and five officers were standing on porches, pounding on doors of church member's homes. Firearms ready, copies of the court warrant brandished, they pushed their way pass the adults, rushed into the homes and seized 112 youngsters under the age of seventeen.

Swiftly, they and state welfare workers inspected and photographed bedrooms and toilets and playrooms to which their access had been denied earlier. Defiant welfare workers gathered dowel rods — proof that the children were regularly spanked.

But by 6:45, the press reported, the mood of the raid

began to change. Law enforcement officers — state troopers and deputies — had been briefed to expect terrified children pleading to be rescued from screeching, cult-crazed mothers and brutal, possibly polygamous fathers. State troopers had been told to expect and overcome organized, armed resistance.

Instead, weeping parents helped their youngsters walk to the buses and prayed over them as their kids boarded the steps.

Calmly, the well-trained, obedient youngsters heeded their tearful parents' instructions to do what the troopers said, to be good — and to trust Jesus.

"Don't worry, Jesus is with you," whispered one mother to her pre-schooler. "You will be home real soon."

Clinging to her, "Mama," cried one little girl, "don't let them take me. I love you. Where are we going?"

"Now, now, now," soothed the mother as an embarrassed trooper averted his eyes. "You just stay with this policeman. He'll take care of you."

Gently, she lifted the little girl up to the tough lawman. The little girl, her face wet with tears, clutched him around the neck.

"Hey, hey," he found himself saying. "You can ride in my car. We're going to take care of you, honey."

Yes, there were young tears. Some of the kids — particularly the little ones — became confused and worried. Wails wafted up, but were gently soothed by the older kids.

These were strong, brave young prayer warriors, used to long hikes in the mountains. Yet, some did look so lost in the hubbub. Many had never been separated from their parents.

Now, they were being snatched from their loving

families by document-waving welfare officials and uniformed lawmen unused to dealing with children. Bewildered, they stared out of the bus windows, their eyes big,
their little hearts breaking.

But older kids started singing choruses.

Parents standing outside the buses sang along and
talked with the littlest, most bewildered ones.

Church members without children gathered in the
church's Maple Hotel, offering intercession unto the
Lord for His swift intervention and protection.

Members of the assembled press marveled as bearded
church members obediently stood beside the buses and
talked gently with their kids or beseeched the Lord at
curbside. A group of fathers asked permission to accom-
pany the kids to wherever it was that the state was going
to take them.

Troopers became angry — but not with the church
members. It had become obvious to police that these
church members were not about to fight back physically.
"Troopers took off their heavy flak jackets and tossed
them into their cruisers," wrote one member of the press.
The officers began "to assume the role that would keep
them busy through a long, confusing day ... a uniformed
force of babysitters."

Local and national news reporters and camera teams
milled, also increasingly irritated. They'd been tipped off
to the raid by the State of Vermont — and told that they
would witness the break-up of another Guyana-type
Jonestown. They grew increasingly impatient that no
"big story" of a cult's bloody resistance to lawmen panned
out.

It has been hypothesized that officials of the State of
Vermont knew perfectly well that the raid on the church

was completely illegal. However, members of the national press were summoned in expectation of a Wounded
Knee, South Dakota-type gunfight by violent, howling
cult defenders and the state's rescue of beaten, bruised
and naked children.

Had any of that happened, grisly photos in the major
newspapers and tear-jerking videotape on TV networks
of battered, sexually exploited youngsters would turn
Vermont officials into national heroes.

But newsmen recorded a completely different scene.
The church's children trooped out to the buses in straight
lines, rosy-cheeked and unafraid. On the buses, they
hung out the windows, obediently listening to their
parents, then began singing children's choruses, led by
the older kids.

Members of the press gathered at the church-owned
hotel and were met by calm, anxious church members
who invited the reporters to join them in praying about
the raid-in-progress — and for God to halt the evil that
was unfolding.

"We are not battling flesh and blood," explained one
soft-spoken church deacon. This battle will be won in the
heavenlies. Watch and see: *our God protects His people.*"

As the stunned press stared, the prayerful non-parents continued to intercede — to beg the Lord for His
protection and provision and intervention.

Yes, these folks were fighters.

But they were also prayer warriors. They truly knew
how to fight back.

With God before them, who could stand against them?

Reporters from NBC, ABC, and CBS News, the Cana-
dian Broadcasting Corporation, the Associated Press,
United Press International, and even the French news

agency Gamma-Liason began asking welfare officials some embarrassing questions.

State officials went into a huddle. Police commanders hotly demanded explanations. Several sheriff's deputies were ready to unload the buses and turn the kids loose. This wasn't the reception they had been told to expect from a bunch of religious hot-heads. These were not para-military fanatics. *These were Christians.*

After the meeting, apologetic Vermont State Police officials announced that as many parents as wished to come could ride with their children on the buses.

Gary Long, a non-parent church member, "waved a cheerful good-bye from the front porch," one reporter wrote. "'Hurry back,' he said. Then still in his bare feet, he stepped out to the street to make one more attempt" to convert the newspaper reporter to Christianity.

By 9 a.m., the kids and many of the parents of Island Pond's Community Church had been taken away on the buses. By 9:30 a.m., they began to fill an emergency "crisis center" at a National Guard armory in the nearby village of Newport.

And God continued to be faithful.

A state judge named Frank Mahady was awakened at home 120 miles away by state prosecutors who had helped organize the raid. The judge who had helped plan the raid had been called away. Officials needed Mahady to be on hand for various legal procedures — such as authorizing the placement of the children in state custody.

Mahady, expecting either a revival of Woodstock or else the horror Jonestown, Guyana, arrived at the Newport County Courthouse and examined a few youngsters.

He became angry at officials who had organized the raid. These were not dirty, abused, neglected kids. These were bright-eyed, sharp, cooperative youngsters — well-fed, well-clothed and completely respectful of his authority. He spurned the necessary court orders put before him to allow 50 doctors, nurses and psychologists to examine and question the children.

Mahady ordered the children returned—*immediately*.

He thundered that there was no cause to detain any of the kids and that the state had ignored both Vermont State Constitution and the U.S. Bill of Rights by instigating the raid.

As TV cameras whirred, state prosecutors put up a humiliating protest. Mahady ignored them, turning to order a court clerk to summon a public defender to represent the children's interests should the state decide to take the case over Mahady's head.

Back in Island Pond, the fervent prayers of intercession and the petition of parents and non-parents grew in intensity.

I want you to understand exactly how this battle was won: *Instead of fearing or fighting, church members trusted in the Lord.*

By now, they were exercising deep faith. No longer could they see the effects of their prayers. No longer could they watch the troopers actually putting down weapons and arguing with welfare workers and state prosecutors.

Now the action was distant — in Newport.

The prayer warriors could not see how the Lord was intervening this time.

They did not know that Mahady's request for a public defender was being given to born-again public defender

Andrew Crane. He rushed to the armory and agreed to defend the 112 youngsters — then refused to sign any papers allowing the kids to be examined or even questioned. He began telephoning his lawyer friends in human rights organizations and even asking for help from associates in the Vermont chapter of the American Civil Liberties Union.

And the ACLU — usually antagonistic to any Christian cause — joined the fight on the side of the church. Before noon, 50 attorneys were on the scene — *fighting for the kids.*

Meanwhile, Judge Mahady was growing increasingly vitriolic in his denunciations of the raid. State welfare officials cowered under his vehement itemizations of their violations of state and federal law. State prosecutors excused themselves to telephones where they requested — but did not receive reinforcements from the state capital.

News of the raid was already on local television.

State officials — particularly elected officials — could see that the situation was souring.

They offered no help. The prosecutors on the scene were on their own.

And with only weak protests from the state prosecutors on the scene, the 112 youngsters were released to their joyful parents.

TV cameras recorded their praises to the Lord, their happy declarations of His mercy, His strength, His power.

One purpose of Vermont's Juvenile Procedures Act, Judge Mahady would declare days later in his formal, multiple-page repudiation of the state's request that the children be put in foster homes, *is to provide for the care, protection and wholesome moral, mental and physical development of children. However, it is the unequivocal goal of the Vermont legislature to achieve this purpose, whenever possible in a family environment — separating the child from his parent only when necessary for his welfare.*

Therefore, it is the burden and heavy responsibility of the state to demonstrate by sufficient evidence, not generalized assumption, that it is necessary to separate each of the 112 children from his or her parents.

The state virtually admits that it cannot meet this burden. Its petition, on its face, does not even allege that the children are, indeed, in need of care and supervision. The allegation is merely a blatantly generalized assumption.

Here the state lacks any proof whatsoever as to these children and these parents, much less convincing proof.

For these reasons, this court refused the state's rather incredible request that the court issue a blanket detention order for 112 children without even holding hearings.

Judge Mahady chastised state prosecutors and welfare workers for attempting to treat the children as "potential pieces of evidence." He stated in his decision:

It was the state's admitted purpose to transport each of the 112 children to a special clinic where they were to be examined by a team of doctors and psychologists for evidence of abuse. If no signs of abuse were found, a child would be returned to his parents, provided the parents "cooperated," that is, gave certain information to the police.

Thus, not only were the children to be treated as mere pieces of evidence, they were also to be held hostage to the ransom demand of information to the parents.

This stated plan of the state lends credence to the complaint of a number of the parents during the course of the hearings to the effect that they had been told by law enforcement personnel at the time of the raid that they would not be reunited with their children unless they gave certain information. During the course of the hearings, the state did indicate that, if custody were awarded, children would be returned to "cooperative parents."

Had the court issued detention orders requested by the state, it would have made itself a party to this grossly unlawful scheme.

What's the bottom line to this incredible tale?

It's how the people of this church fought back.

With humble petitions to the Most High.

With prayer.

With trust in the Lord.

Even secular reporters came away astonished with the peace of these folks — their trust in the Lord's deliverance.

The children are dancing, wrote one reporter, Jim Kenary, *and the adults are sitting around them in a circle, singing. In one corner several people are playing instruments — guitars, tambourines, a piano. I look for a leader, someone who might be directing the service, but it seems to be happening on its own.*

One woman stands and reads from her Bible, looking up occasionally to describe the passage in her own words. She is explaining to the group that her love for Jesus is so strong, so absolute that on Friday when the police entered her home and threatened to take her children away from her, she was prepared to let them go if God desired it. Other members nod vehemently and utter 'Amen.'

"Another man rises and describes the peacefulness

that came over him as the police stormed into his house early Friday morning. Reaching into the air, as if he is clutching for something, he tells his brothers and sisters about the time in his life when he might have reacted violently, when he might have fought back. But now, he says, he can feel nothing but compassion and love, and overwhelming peace.

"They go on and on. The proclamations seem endless. As many women stand up to speak as men. This surprises me considering the covered heads and the belief in submission. Someone tells the story of how several state troopers had apologized to the church members for what they were having to do on the day of the raid. One trooper had proclaimed himself 'a born-again Christian.' Another had told certain church members that he would allow them to babysit his two-month-old daughter any time…"

What has happened within the hierarchy of the state of Vermont? The State Attorney General was soundly defeated in his bid to become the next governor of Vermont.

All charges against the church members were dropped.

Some state officials still grumble about the embarrassing defeat. "There are careers on the line," quipped attorney Scott Skinner, who remains friends with the kids he defended.

"Like the martyrs we all learned about in Sunday school, the bearded, long-haired men and kerchiefed, skirted women had maintained a calm dignity during their eighteen-hour ordeal," read one news account. *"They displayed neither anger nor hysteria as they delivered their children over to the state; or as they led and carried them across Newport's Main Street through a gauntlet of state police, reporters, photographers and, as the long*

day turned into night, the glare of television lights.

"In court, according to defense attorney Richard Rubin, they 'presented themselves with a dignity and humility' which he found remarkable in view of the stress they were undergoing.

"As they emerged from the Orleans County Courthouse, some of them told their children to smile. And the children, looking heartbreakingly innocent and vulnerable, smiled as the state troopers ushered them back across the street and into the waiting buses.

"Now they were taking their children home. Behind them they left some of Vermont's highest officials, men of considerable power, who had spent all afternoon standing on the sidewalks in front of the courthouse, watching and waiting while a bold, well-planned and deftly executed operation crumbled into a stunning defeat.

"They had been beaten."

That's what happens, my friends, when we Christians fight back with the weapons that our great God gives us.

The State of Vermont expected the members of the church to come out with guns ablaze. Ungodly officials just weren't prepared for the manner in which the Christians would go over their heads — straight to the throne of the Creator.

Members of the Island Pond church had been taught exactly how to do battle.

On their knees.

It works, my friend.

2

Kids Fighting Back

Your kids need to know how to fight back, too.

Don't think for a minute that there weren't some pint-sized Christians interceding on those buses at Island Pond.

The Lord hears the honest, trusting prayers of the innocent child. Jesus made repeated references in the Gospels to the special place in His heart that God has for kids. One passage says their "angels" have instant access to the Father.

So, there are all sorts of good reasons to teach your kids to trust the Lord for daily help.

It may save their lives.

Ron was filled with a horrifying premonition that his five-year-old kindergartner was in danger.

He and I had been involved in some particularly heavy spiritual warfare as we researched and polished the last chapters of my book *Devil on the Run*. For example, his employer, the publishing company releasing the book was battling an incredible demonic attack — an assault it would not survive.

How could the Lord let a Christian publisher fall into bankruptcy? Well, that's another story I will tell in detail at another time. But the bottom line is that amid that spiritual battle, the owner made several critical misjudgments. Perhaps the deciding one was when he consciously chose to depend on a man, an "expert," instead of Jesus Christ — a move that I cautioned him strongly against.

In Isaiah 31:1, we are warned: "Woe to those who go down to Egypt for help, who rely on horses and trust in chariots ... [but] look not to the Holy One of Israel, nor seek and consult the Lord!"

So, the Lord let that publishing company fail despite record sales and a promising future.

I hate to be too critical of anyone's weakness of faith. It's too easy a cop-out: "She wasn't healed because she lacked faith" or "His company didn't survive the recession because they didn't have enough faith." But here was a company besieged on every side — with an owner trying to fight in his own strength and listening too much to advisors who were skeptical of the modern realities of spiritual warfare.

You and I live in a world that often hides its head in the sand when it comes to spiritual battle.

"Rational" people do not admit belief in the supernatural. Some good Christians will tell you bluntly that all miracles and all demon-possession ended suddenly after the time of Christ.

A recent news magazine article poked fun at the idea of demon-possession today. "For most ... exorcism belongs in the shadows of their church's distant past," wrote reporters Bill Turque and Farai Chideya. "As medicine and psychiatry began to explain the demons that produce mental illness, the ritual became a rarity, confined largely to supermarket tabloids and Hollywood scripts ...." (Quoted from "The Exorcism of Gina," *Newsweek,* Vol. CXVII, No. 15, pg. 62)

Amid the turmoil of his employer struggling to remain solvent, the battle to finish *Devil on the Run* intensified. During his private, morning prayer times, Ron became increasingly concerned for the personal safety of his little girl.

As we worked on *Devil on the Run,* Ron and I had examined quite a number of horrible, true stories of Satanists shedding the blood of the young and innocent in their evil rites.

Then, he began to hear local stories going around about unsolved child abductions and satanic sacrifices of little children.

So, you can understand why Ron paid attention to the Lord's gentle warning that something terrible was interested in his daughter. Seeking the Lord, Ron became filled with a deep sense of urgency to intercede for the safety of his little girl.

This child, Amelia, was a big-eyed, trusting child with a deep empathy for others. She felt others' pain. Her father knew that of his four kids, she was the one that would be tragically terrorized by any evil-doers delighting in the horror of a small child.

Her feisty older sister, Jan, would put up a battle. Her tough little brother, Rupert, would let out a belligerent howl. And littlest brother Nicholas was just a baby who would cry if anybody he didn't know came near him.

But five-year-old Amelia would just be petrified and

absolutely intimidated — which would thrill anyone thriving on the terror of innocents.

As Amelia's father wrestled with this strange foreboding, he was unaware that his wife had also had the same terrible warning. She, too, had discerned the Lord telling her that some deep, insidious evil wanted Amelia.

Since the warning was so strange, neither parent wanted to mention it to the other — for fear of alarming their spouse. But both parents took the matter to God, pleading for Amelia's safety, protection and provision. Both parents wrestled with talking about such a sudden and very oddball fear — that something evil and dark wanted their little girl.

It was just too weird.

Yet, both parents grew to see that their warning was so strong that it was to be taken seriously — particularly when it became obvious that their little girl had received the very same warning.

Suddenly the child refused to go out into the front yard alone. She worried at bedtime that something was going to get her — and pleaded with her parents to "check on me" after bedtime — then would get up to chastise them for not sticking their heads in her door frequently to make sure she was okay.

Increasingly concerned in his prayer time, Ron felt strongly that he was supposed to talk with little Amelia about his warning and her new fear.

But how?

He swallowed his pride and told his wife about what he had been praying.

"I've had the same thing!" she exclaimed. "And have you noticed how scared Amelia is lately? Something has her really spooked."

Together, they agreed in prayer, just as Matthew 18:19 tells us, that the Father would protect their little girl. Then, the dad went to talk to Amelia about all this.

But what was he supposed to say to a tender kindergartner? He couldn't warn her that there are terrible people out there who love abusing innocent little girls or whose dark rituals demand the sacrifice of a terrified child.

No, he had to assure her.

But how could he do it honestly?

He knew he could not merely tell her to depend on her daddy to come protect her. If, indeed, something great and evil snatched her away, the evil tormentors would just delight in a little girl crying out for her daddy — *a human daddy who could not come.*

Instead, he knew, Amelia needed to know the great power of her true Protector. The child had to understand that her great Father was ready to come to her aid whenever she called for His help.

"Honey," Ron told his little girl that evening as he held her in his arms, "You know that your mom and I love you very much."

Amelia smiled, her face aglow with her love for her daddy.

"Did you know that Jesus cares about you very much, too?"

"Oh, yes," answered the kindergartner.

"Did you know that He will protect you?"

She nodded, happily.

"Amelia," said her dad softly. "You know that if anything bad ever tried to hurt you, I would fight for you. But what are you supposed to do if I'm not around?"

"Get mommy?" answered his daughter.

"What if she's not around?"

"Get somebody else?"

"Well," said Ron, "Do you know who can defeat anything bad that might try to get you?"

"Jesus!"

"That's right. He can fight off stuff that your daddy can't even see. He can protect you when you don't even know that something is waiting for you."

Solemnly the little girl nodded — remembering a Sunday school lesson. "I need to say 'In Jesus' name you bad person leave me alone!'"

Amelia's dad smiled, fighting sudden emotion. "That's right. Jesus will help you when Daddy can't. Jesus can tell Daddy or Mommy to come help. And Jesus can keep *anything* bad from touching you."

The kindergartner blinked solemnly.

"I'm going to ask Jesus to help me when I'm scared," she said, yawning sleepily.

And secure in her Daddy's arms, Amelia drifted off to sleep.

Weeks later, on the morning of October 31, Ron was filled with a sudden, new concern. In his morning prayer time, he fell on his face before the Lord — seeking safety for his beloved little girl.

This dad knew, somehow deep within his spirit, that this was the day.

Halloween. October 31 — All Hallowed's Eve. *Devil's Night.*

In faith, he thanked the Lord for surrounding his darling child with a great force of angels — and for fighting back any evil that wanted to destroy Amelia's innocence and joy.

And he prayed a new prayer that the Lord had stirred

within him — asking for intercessors. He asked God to send people who would spontaneously be urged to pray on his and his family's behalf.

That Halloween morning, his wife was also stirred in her morning quiet time that this was the day she'd been warned about. She, too, petitioned the Lord to protect all of her kids — and particularly Amelia. Then, the mom was stirred to ask God to surround their home with a spiritual "hedge of thorns" that Satan's evil could not penetrate.

At peace, both parents went about their day.

Yet as Halloween evening neared, both were repeatedly stirred in their spirits to offer sincere intercession for Amelia.

Both knew something was up.

As sundown neared, Amelia's tomboy sister was playing on a skateboard in the driveway of a vacant house next door. She was excited about that evening's Harvest Celebration party at church — a four-hour, safe alternative to trick-or-treating.

As she zoomed down the driveway, a dark sedan slowed on the busy boulevard next to the neighborhood. The older girl squinted and grew concerned that three people in black clothes and strange facial paint were looking her over. She decided to ignore them.

Then, across the lawn, Amelia came marching.

"Mommy says you're not supposed to be out of the yard!" called the little sister. "I'm gonna tell!"

The car screeched to a stop.

A black-garbed figure leaped out — and ran toward Amelia.

Frozen, Amelia stared in terror, then spun and ran toward the house.

As her older sister began screaming for help at the top of her lungs, the kindergartner dashed for her safety. "Mommy, Mommy, Mommy!" Amelia screamed.

Her mom ran outside, and she saw an incredible sight.

A black-clothed figure was in hot pursuit of her daughter — arms outstretched to grab the little girl.

But suddenly she reached the property line.

And the dark figure stopped cold ... as if there were an invisible hedge of thorns surrounding the yard.

In the darkening street, the car's engine roared.

The black-clothed figure turned, ran to the car and jumped in. In a squeal of rubber, the car sped off.

As Amelia wept, her mom sprinted out into the street and memorized the license tag. Grabbing Amelia, she ran inside and dialed "911."

Within moments, the street was filled with police cars and motorcycles.

Not mentioning their weeks of warning, Amelia's mother calmly explained what had just occurred.

Amelia's big sister told what she had seen.

And big-eyed Amelia excitedly told her story.

"They tried to *get* me!" she protested. "Bad people! A witch!"

The officers fell in love with the long-haired kindergartner. They knelt around her, gently asking her details of what had happened. They praised her for doing all the right things.

They smiled as she declared that Jesus had protected her — just like her daddy had said He would.

"What a darling child," whispered an enormous patrolman to Amelia's mom as he finished writing his report. "This is no ordinary little girl."

A half hour later, police brought back a black-garbed

figure. The teenager mumbled an apology to Amelia and her mother. As the teen slouched in the living room, Amelia's mother sensed a terrible evil — that troubled her deeply.

"It was apparently just a Halloween prank," said the investigating officer. "I don't believe we should bring charges. But we will keep an eye on this teen."

That evening, little Amelia dressed up as a lion from Daniel's den and happily trooped off to the church Harvest Celebration.

She seemed to have forgotten the entire thing.

But her parents knew what had happened.

They had fought back.

And they had won.

Today Amelia is a bright-eyed, faith-filled child, whose parents would prefer not to recount her Halloween misadventure. There are more important things to fill her world, such as Bible stories, baby dolls and bicycles.

Occasionally, she will become afraid for no apparent reason — and will balk at running an errand outside unless one of her parents is watching from the door.

The battle for the publishing company was lost, of course. Many good people lost their jobs. Others would lose lots of money. But the evil did not touch *Devil on the Run.* Another strong, reputable publisher, New Leaf Press, stepped in to keep it and my other books in print.

Devil on the Run has gone on to sell many thousands of copies, and continues to do so. Little Amelia's daddy went on to work for my new publisher.

And Amelia continues to grow strong in the Lord, a charming child full of faith — who knows the source of her true protection.

3

Witches in our Midst

Mannatu Crossing is a little tourist spot on the highway up in New England's mountains — an unincorporated settlement with a tantalizing, occult heritage.

The word "mannatu" is an Algonquin Indian word for a vengeful demon that supposedly lurks in bewitched New England rocks, springs or groves. At least one movie and an episode of the old TV horror series *The Night Stalker* dealt with a murderous mannatu (sometimes spelled "manitou") intent on bloody devastation.

Local New Agers scoff at such notions and note that a mannatu can also be a benevolent spirit, a spiritual force of nature, or a guardian of the ecology — the healer through the waters.

And that may give you an idea of this quaint settlement the day Pastor Tom and his wife, Leisha, moved in. Yuppie tourists were milling about spending their monies on everything from ice-cream to fine art. The beautiful mountains glistened on the horizon.

I'll never forget the day I met Tom and Leisha. I was holding a seminar at a nearby retreat center and had decided I really needed to get away and go sweat at a spa and hot springs I had seen advertised on the highway.

I was sitting there in the steam relaxing when an outspoken man entered. He was dark-skinned and athletic in build. I thought perhaps he was Italian from nearby New York City.

I wondered what his trouble must be as I observed him talking with the attendant. His talkative manner made way for a conversation. "What type of work do you do?" he asked me.

"I'm an author."

"Where are you from?"

"New York," I told him.

His evangelistic nature took over. I realized he was trying to witness to me when he asked if I'd ever heard of the book, *The Cross and the Switchblade*.

With a chuckle, I said, "Yeah, I've heard of it."

We moved on to the whirlpool where I met his wife, a tall, thin blonde in a modest swim suit.

She asked, "What is your name?"

"Nicky Cruz," I replied.

Her face lit up in astonishment as she gave Tom a quick elbow to the ribs. "Don't you know who this is?" she asked Tom.

And that was the beginning of a friendship God had appointed. Tom and Leisha had just moved from their home in Yonkers after two years of planning to obey the voice of God telling them to relocate. The Lord had instructed Tom that they were to plant a church. They had been evangelists for years. What did they know about church planting? What did they know about pastoring?

One thing I found they did know about was the occult and the powerful forces of evil.

At least they thought they did.

Tom had conducted seminars in nearly every denomination for the past four years on the occult, rock music, and false religions. They were accustomed to threats, spiritual warfare, and being confronted with evil. They knew all about how to fight back ... so they thought.

So, at Mannatu Crossing, they began a Bible study in their small apartment with one young girl. The Bible study grew and they soon began to meet in the apartment clubhouse adjacent to the pool, where many were baptized.

With twenty-five attending, they began to pray for a building to meet in — and be a real church.

One young man who'd been saved and baptized through their ministry introduced Tom and Leisha to his father, a spirit-filled Christian who'd prayed for his son's salvation for years. He was so overjoyed that his son had come to the Lord that he asked Tom and Leisha what he could do to help their ministry.

They informed him they were looking for a place to meet. The man happened to own an old, run-down building with lots of space — a virtual hole in the wall. He offered to let them meet there free of charge.

What he neglected to mention was how he'd had a terrible time running off a demonic group that had been meeting in the abandoned building.

Not your ordinary occultists, this group prayed to the ancient *mannatu* of the area which they believed was the ancient Indian spirit healer of the mountain waters.

The *mannatu*.

The demon of the local springs.

The demonic spirit of Mannatu Crossing.

What a terrible heritage. What horrible power it can wreak over an entire area. The town could not shed the occult darkness of its founding fathers.

So often, I see the truth of the Bible's references to the "sins of the fathers" affecting the lives of the sons. In the same way, the area around Virginia Beach, Virginia, has been blessed by God — perhaps because the original settlers at Cape Henry dedicated the area to the spreading of the gospel.

And so it has been with tiny little Mannatu Crossing, except that its heritage is dark, evil and sinister.

Tom and Leisha soon learned the hard way the power behind the evil, vengeful spirit of the bubbling New England springs.

Ever since Revolutionary War days, there's been a powerful demonic hold over the area, attracting mystics and spiritualists, city folks seeking an occult experience, wanting to commune with the dark forces of the unknown. In Mannatu Crossing they could be accepted.

Annually the area has a big "psychic fair" well attended by tourists from Boston and New York City and Philadelphia. There, for $30, you can sit down across a table from a palm reader or a crystal-ball fortune-teller or a tea-leaves reader.

The old building Tom and Leisha were lent was old, I mean old ... spooky and run down, but it was free and it was a place to start for their church.

Tom began putting up posters around and in the nearby incorporated townships, announcing a seminar on the occult and rock music. That would surely attract people, he felt.

Indeed it did.

People were used to going to Mannatu Crossing to dabble in the weird.

One character who showed up came in black leather, dark sunglasses, dyed black hair, and inverted crosses around his neck. During greetings he avoided everyone, grumbled through the presentation and kept one hand inside his jacket as if clutching a weapon. Tom instructed an usher to sit next to him for fear he might start shooting into the crowd. When the altar call came, he made the quickest dart for the door and ran down the sidewalk and disappeared into the darkness as if he had dissipated with it. Tom and Leisha never saw him again.

You see, they were in a war zone. Their church sat smack dab in the middle of a satanic high priest's turf. They have territories they spiritually rule over — territories that are literally marked off on the map. The new church happened to sit in the middle of one of the most evil, high honcho's perverse parishes.

This high priest was so jealous of his evil territory that he had people assigned to walk around the entire circumference praying to the devil, daily.

Until Tom and Leisha came along he'd had free reign. They later discovered that four churches had previously failed — shut their doors — in that same building.

Now spiritually, after one generational Satanist (someone whose parents had been Satanists, too) was converted and when a former witch became a Christian, the church began to pose a real threat!

Spray-painted messages in blood red began to appear on the church windows. "We've come for your children!"

appeared across the large pane glass which faced the congregation during worship. Each service Tom and Leisha would arrive early and sure enough, there would be a new message ... and they'd hurry and try to scrape it off prior to the service.

Tom and Leisha knew they were at war!

Then the bomb threats began. After the first one, police evacuated the entire building. They searched for hours, finding nothing.

"Oh, just another nut case ..." was one officer's comment during the ordeal. Tom and Leisha soon learned not to expect much help from local law enforcement agencies. Most of what was occurring, the official attitude seemed to be, was that mischievous teens were pulling benign pranks on an excitable bunch of religious zealots who probably were some sort of cult themselves.

Then, two of the men caught spray-painting the church windows were in their early thirties. Not long after that, members' car window were bashed with baseball bats during a service.

Instead of doubling their efforts to protect church members, the police turned hostile. Deputies made no pretense of the fact that they were tired of running out to Mannatu Crossing to chase shadows.

Since there were no Satanists to tongue-lash, they took their frustration out on the church members, advising them that they must be doing *something* to bring on such trouble. It had to stop, officers advised privately. Enough was enough.

It was about then that Tom called an all-night prayer meeting at the church. The turnout was good despite growing fear among members.

But the next morning, all of the people's cars had been

ticketed by county deputies for parking violations. Enormous fines were incurred. The message: *we're tired of this trouble — why don't you people just quit? Back off!*

Tom began to feel serious paranoia. Then he realized: It was perfectly sane to worry that everybody around was out to get him — because they really were!

In the next weeks:

• the church's mail began to disappear;

• county and state officials began inspecting their building for health and fire code violations — and each time, the church was required to make expensive, but petty alterations;

• their bank account got tangled up — with deposits being listed as withdrawals and quite a number of checks bouncing to the extreme embarrassment of Tom and Leisha;

• vandalism increased to members' homes and to the church property.

Tom and Leisha always wondered why the Lord gave them such a tough spiritual assignment. They've come to learn why. This has made them strong. You must be strong to stand against evil. You must know who you are in God. You must be strong in the Power within you.

You must know … *that you know.*

And why you know it.

You must be as firm as a rock, unmovable, standing your ground with all firmness, with full confidence in God and who He really is. All power is given unto you! Demonized agents of hell are wimps in the presence of God! Their bluff is a whimper in the face of the Almighty!

There's no place in this war for spinelessness or weakness. No place for even flirting with the idea of sin.

Holiness is a must, it could mean your life.

You have to be blameless.

Hey, that's no easy task for we mere humans.

I sin.

I do. So do you, whether you like to admit it or not. Occasionally, I yell at my wife when I should be patient and understanding. And I don't grab every opportunity to witness to every airline hostess and hotel bellman.

I am not perfect.

But I have learned that I have to be so careful. I must not let greed slip in and ruin my testimony. I must fight pride sneaking in to undermine my ministry!

You and I can't cheat on our taxes, because if we are really threatening his unholy kingdom, Satan will be waiting and watching. He will know and see! Experience has shown us all that the Lord will let us suffer the earthly consequences of such sin!

The Lord loved King David dearly. But He allowed David to suffer the earthly consequences of committing adultery with another man's wife.

The Lord dearly loved Adam and Eve. But He allowed them to suffer the consequences of chomping down on that forbidden apple.

And you and I can name two or three great preachers, soul-winners and televangelists who fell into sin — and who the Lord allowed to suffer human and legal consequences of their sin.

If you are battling Satan's kingdom effectively, but cheat on your 1040, before you know it, the IRS will be on your doorstep with the *New York Daily News, 60-Minutes,* Geraldo Rivera and CNN! The Lord will stand back and Satan will barge in like a steam roller!

Tom and Leisha learned some hard lessons.

And when they resisted terrible temptations to sin, he

tried their finances, their stamina, their spirits, even their health.

I don't believe that every sickness and disease results from direct demonic attack. Some are the consequences of our own neglect and some are the consequences of the sinful world we live in. But it was a direct attack by Satan when Leisha burned her arm.

She was cooking on the stove with oil and received a phone call. She thought she had turned the oil off to cool, but had actually turned it up.

When she hung up and grabbed the hot skillet, she splashed hot grease over her right hand and arm. She immediately screamed in an agony that actually found her writhing on the kitchen floor. She began to tremble. A cold sweat broke out and her vision became blurred.

She crawled to the phone and dialed the church office. It was busy! "What should I do?" she thought as she was losing consciousness. She dialed the phone again and, instead, got the Christian businessman who owned the building

Leisha screamed something unintelligible. He got the message that something was definitely wrong.

Leisha lay there on the kitchen floor in near-shock. Tom soon arrived. She spent that night in tormenting pain — but didn't require hospitalization even though she had third-degree burns. In fact, she was nearly recovered by the weekend.

On Sunday, Tom and Leisha arrived early for church as usual to check things over. One of the top drug dealers of a large nearby town who was a well known Satanist was waiting by the door.

They wondered what he was up to.

Perhaps he'll get saved today, they thought. As they

got out of the car, he made a beeline for Leisha. Nodding at her bandages, he sweetly inquired, "What happened to you?"

"I burned myself."

"I know!" he sneered, with an evil grin. Then, he broke into a hysterical laugh.

Quickly Leisha rebuked him in the Name of Jesus. He turned and strutted away.

Then, one evening, Tom and Leisha were called to the church by their landlord. This kind and loving man of God was distraught as he led them to the church office to show them the handiwork of a man he'd caught breaking in.

Leisha sighed as if a weight had dropped on her chest. Her desk was a mess! Papers were scattered everywhere, torn and smeared with toothpaste. The large picture window behind the desk was smeared with the white, pepperminty goo and some of Tom's sermon notes were plastered to the window with it.

Overturned potted plants and dirt were everywhere! The sight was so disheartening!

Daily there were surprises like this.

As the membership began dropping, Tom had to get two outside jobs to keep the church afloat financially.

Then their four-year-old son, Josh was with Leisha at their office one day and left the office to go to the bathroom in the hallway.

Leisha heard an all too familiar scream and jumped from her chair. She looked down the hallway only to catch a glimpse of a woman dropping Josh from around her waist and running away. Josh came running into the office and hugged his mom has hard as he could.

"Mommy, that mean lady held me really hard," wept

the little boy. "She started to carry me off, but I did like you said. I screamed and kicked and rebuked her in the name of Jesus."

Leisha describes that moment as one which will never slip from her memory.

She decided enough was enough.

This was too much.

They could not touch Josh.

It was time to give up.

Oh, the argument she had with God.

Had He sent her here to sacrifice her family — literally? But Josh's bright and innocent eyes and his loud, proud, repeated descriptions of his brave, determined fight he'd put up and how Jesus had saved him sparked hope in her.

Oh, if we could all have such child-like faith

"I did what you said, and it worked!" exclaimed the little boy.

Yes, it does.

And that's the key, just doing, daily what the Father tells you.

Obedience.

Believing if He said it, it will work.

He is who He says He is!

4

Fighting in God's Strength?

In the next tough months, Psalm 5:11 and 12 gave great strength to Tom and Leisha, "But let all those that put their trust in thee rejoice: let them ever shout for joy, because thou defendest them: let them also that love thy name be joyful in thee. For thou, Lord, wilt bless the righteous; with favor wilt thou compass him with a shield."

What were Tom and Leisha fighting?

Occultists, satanists, witches — bonafide ones — real practitioners of the dark arts.

Yes they do exist.

They are real people like you and I

Some that came against Tom and Leisha were modern-day witches, followers of the "old religion," *wicca* — Earth-mother followers who lived in nearby caves. Some held professional jobs in the city.

One group was quite well off financially and was underwriting members' college education — with the stated intent of placing witches in positions of power and influence in the media.

As Tom and Leisha witnessed publicly, led seminars on the deception of the occult and confronted some very oddball opponents, they were amazed at the diversity of people involved in the darkness.

But Tom and Leisha had a weapon that the Druids, Rosicrucians, necromancers, Taoists, Sikhs, psychics, ESTers, theosophists, astrologers, *ganja*-smokers, Zen nuns, gnostics, wiccans and transcendental meditators lacked: *love.*

Tom and Leisha prayed for a Jesus-type love for even the worst troublemakers.

And they found the occultists had one thing in common, all had been hurt very deeply at one time by Christians, were a bit vengeful, but were seeking fulfillment in life and "cosmic truth."

Hey, there's nothing wrong with cosmic truth. Let me lay a cosmic truth on you: *Almighty God alone created the cosmos, including you, and loves you so much that he sent His own Son to be misunderstood and martyred on your behalf so that you could know His love, accept His love and spend all of eternity enveloped in His love!*

Most of these people were wary of Christians. "I wanted to know the truth," each said in one way or another, as they explained their path into Zen or wicca or astrology or numerology or spiritualism. "This works. Christianity doesn't!"

They were deceived — tricked into believing they'd found real truth, because their occultic mysticism provided excitement and visions and "enlightenment."

They'd gotten none of that at the dead churches of their childhood.

I understand.

As a kid, I hated church. I was occasionally dragged off to high mass on Holy Days, such as Christmas.

And I also used to peek in at my father's demonic ceremonies back in the rural forests of our Caribbean island, Puerto Rico. Dramatic, impressive stuff happened there all the time. Amid downright extraordinary hocus-pocus, my dad would order demons out and weird little frogs would squeeze out of people's infected legs and crawl away into the darkness.

As you may have read in my book about my wild childhood, *Devil on the Run,* he'd send evil spirits out of sick people and into my mother — and she'd scream and curse and yell all sorts of hellish stuff as he ordered the demon back to hell.

After she became a Christian, we talked about those years. It was no act, she told me. She was not putting on a show. Great, terrible beings overtook her mind and body. And they only left when my father ordered them away.

And because my dad was not a Christian, much worse stuff took the place of the evil exorcised.

So, I know that this stuff is not just parlor tricks. It can be very, very real. Satan does have power. Why else do you think the Bible is so sternly against witchcraft? If it was just sleight of hand, wires and mirrors, King Saul would not have lost his kingdom for visiting a witch.

No, the New Testament lists witchcraft right up there with murder and adultery.

It's real.

Powerful.

Dangerous.

And forbidden.

But God is more powerful. He always wins, too.

So, if your interest is only on being on the winning team, forget Satanism. The Almighty God who created the Archangel Lucifer can and will someday banish him and all his minions forever into the lake of fire from which they will never again emerge.

Lucifer, Satan, Beelzebub — whatever you want to call the devil — already tried once to invade heaven and wrestle control away from God.

But it was like a five-year-old trying to take over his kindergarten. He might put up a loud squawk, but guess who wins? The teacher!

But that doesn't prevent some five-year-olds from trying. And it's the same with Satan. In his great rebellion and bitterness, he likes to cause as much chaos, pain and destruction as possible — even though he knows he's already lost the battle.

Such was the attack against Tom and Leisha's little evangelistic outreach. Satan could not win.

But he sure could make a mess of things.

With their church under nasty attack, it continued to grow anyway — to fifty-two members. Many were former occultists, convinced by Tom and Leisha's patient love of the true power of the Holy Spirit. They saw that our Creator is more powerful and certainly much more loving than Satan.

The demonic demonstrations they'd seen paled in comparison to the joy and peace that Jesus gave them — and the power that grew within them through the Holy Spirit.

Then Leisha had a dream.

In it she and Tom were invited to dinner at a member's home. Leisha wasn't sure who it was, she just knew it was someone they counted upon a lot — who served in the church.

Upon Tom and Leisha's arrival, the couple gave them a tour of their home, but when they came to the master bedroom, the woman blocked the entrance and made a comment to the fact that she "had run out of time in my cleaning today and didn't get to that room and would rather you not see it."

Everyone just laughed it off and proceeded to the back yard where a barbecue was planned.

Leisha, in her dream, left the yard and entered the house to find the bathroom. Becoming disoriented in the house she mistakenly opened the master bedroom door. To her surprise, a Satanic altar was arrayed with candles burning, a human skull and large pentagram filling one entire wall of the bedroom.

In horror, Leisha awoke from the dream. She shook Tom and they prayed for discernment and wisdom.

She knew it was from the Lord.

However, discerning the real meaning of the dream was another matter. Did it mean that somebody in the church was really a Satanist? Or was it symbolic? Or maybe it was a deception from the devil to make them suspect a godly friend. Perhaps it was just too much pizza the night before.

No, Tom and Leisha had a deep conviction that the dream was real, from the Lord — and to be heeded.

It was a difficult time for the young couple — they couldn't allow a spirit of fear to overtake them or for suspicion to rob them of freedom and fellowship.

Through intense prayer and fasting, they were shown the infiltrator.

Infiltration is a common tactic among occultists. They

send a member into a church that has posed a threat —
such as a church reaching teens who have been attracted
into the dark arts. I know of instances when witches sent
someone who looked like a Christian, acted like one,
talked the talk, seemingly walked the walk, and even
knew the Bible better than you or me.

They become the best servant you have in the church.
They bring people to the church, they win your heart and
then ... from the inside out they destroy the congregation.
Their first tactic is to rip it apart with their tongue —
with gossip and back-biting and rumors and accusations.

How can you fight back against this sort of attack? The
world is supposed to know we are Christians by our love
— not by our paranoia! Back in American history, some
sincere believers in Salem, Massachusetts, got caught
up in this problem. As a result, apparently, they bar-
becued some innocent girls in their too-zealous desire to
obey the Bible.

And today, if we believe that Jesus came for the lost,
we can't just toss out every gossip for being a suspected
witch!

Tom and Leisha found that — just as in her dream —
one of their members had been destroying the church
behind their backs. He did entertain in his home. He
served up scrumptious meals with a big dessert of gossip
and dissension — tearing away at the authority of the
pastor, at the order of the church, at the beautiful
worship of the Lord, at anything that stood for order.

And he was a practicing Satanist — just like Leisha
had seen in her dream.

So, how do you expel a Satanist from your church?
After all, didn't Jesus come for the sinners? Didn't
He rebuke the religious leaders of His time when

they criticized the way he liked to mingle with the street people, prostitutes and dregs of society? Luke 5:30-31 tells how the Pharisees were grumbling, "Why are you eating and drinking with tax collectors and sinful people?"

Jesus replied to them, "It is not those who are healthy who need a physician, but those who are sick."

So, just because Tom had discovered that he had a practicing Satanist in his midst who was intent on destroying the church ... what could Tom do?

Well, as you may have read in my book *Destined to Win,* we Christians are obligated to follow some truly excellent guidelines for dealing with an unrepentant troublemaker.

The bottom line is that we are required to be merciful.

First, we are to go privately to the offender and give him or her every benefit of the doubt. Matthew 18:15 and Romans 14:1 and Galatians 5:10 leave very little to the imagination. I must go to my brother privately and counsel him — telling him what I think he did wrong. I am to do so humbly — with the distinct possibility that I don't know what I'm talking about.

If he repents, I am to forgive and forget, according to 1 Thessalonians 5:14 and 2 Corinthians 2:6-11.

If he makes a good case that he didn't do anything wrong, you have two options. You can drop it, accepting that you were wrong.

According to Matthew 18:16, you also can go back to him with one or two witnesses and hear his case a second time. Don't take your trigger-happy best friend, either — or somebody who is excited about nailing this troublemaker to the wall.

Take some solid, Bible-reading, on-his-knees disciple

of Jesus Christ — somebody bold enough in the Lord to
tell you to apologize and leave your brother alone.
Taking two witnesses is an even better idea— assuming
you want to be fair and are not just interested in a
spiritual lynching party.

Even better, take an elder or deacon or pastor of your
congregation — somebody in good standing and in authority.

Incidentally, if you are doing this trying to satisfy a
grudge or are seeking personal gain or are trying to win
at church politics, you are asking for big spiritual trouble.
Matthew, Mark and Luke are as blunt as possible about
what God thinks of a Christian who would knowingly
hurt another Christian — and cause him to give up his
faith: "...it would be better for him to have a great
millstone fastened around his neck and to be sunk in the
depth of the sea," says Matthew 18:6.

If your witnesses agree he is wrong, and if he refuses
to listen to them, you can take the matter before the
church, according to Matthew 18:17. Here's where it is
best if one of your witnesses is the pastor or an elder.
Nobody is anxious to haul a fellow believer before a
church tribunal. In this day and age, everybody involved
could be sued for libel, slander and defamation of character. So, it's best if one of your witnesses is a person of
authority who will have the right to decide whether the
whole congregation needs to get dragged into this matter.

Then, what happens?

Matthew here really isn't clear about balloting
or voting somebody out of the church — although
today each group has its own traditions and interpre-
tations. But here's what it says: "...if he refuses to listen

even to the church, let him be to you as a pagan" (Matt. 18:17b).

So, it would seem that if the offender refuses to listen to the authority of the church leaders and/or congregation, he is to be treated like an unbeliever.

And how do we treat unbelievers?

We are to love them and try to convince them of the error of their ways.

Further, if somebody is brought before the church, 2 Corinthians 2:7-8 tells how we are to treat them. After somebody is censured by the majority, "you should turn and forgive and comfort and encourage him to keep him from being overwhelmed by excessive sorrow and despair.

"I therefore beg you to reinstate him in your affections and assure him of your love."

So, it's acceptable to remove that person from the fellowship of the believers while you work on him. 1 Thessalonians says that we are to be patient with such. 2 Thessalonians 3:6, 14 and 15 caution us not to associate with him. But we are not to brand him as our enemy, but admonish him as a brother.

So, with all this in mind, what do you do about a practicing witch in your midst — one who is trying to destroy the church?

When Tom caught onto what was occurring in his church, his only chance was to confront the offender, one-on-one!

You must confront such evil face-to-face, head on! The Lord gave us a full armor, but none for our back side! There is no room for a coward, for running away. Confrontation is a must! Tom confronted the guy — telling him what he suspected.

The troublemaker laughed in his face.

It became obvious that he wanted Tom to throw him out of the church, to kick him out in the name of the Lord, so he could stir up a big fuss!

He wanted to prove to the gawking community that these newcomer Christians are all talk and no love.

He wanted to demonstrate that Jesus Christ has no authority, no power, no ability to handle evil.

So, Tom had quite an assignment:

- He had to get the trouble out of his church
- He had to be strong and justified.
- And he, *absolutely, had to do it in love.*

He took one of the church elders with him and again confronted the troublemaker with the facts:

- That he was constantly gossiping,
- That he seemed to be following an agenda — inviting every member of the church to dinner, then getting them all riled up against the pastor, the order of worship, nit-picking details of theology and outright gossip. Some of it was juicy stuff — that so-and-so was being audited by the IRS, that this or that couple was having marital problems, that somebody else had smoked marijuana with her teenage son when he was 12 — that sort of thing.
- And that there were rumors that the troublemaker, indeed, had an altar to Satan in his master bedroom.

The troublemaker laughed in their faces, then spat this threat: "Just try and kick me out. I'll rip your little church to pieces."

Sure enough, when they had a congregational meeting on the issue, the troublemaker invited the press. He brought his lawyer. And he put on a performance that would have won him an Oscar. He wept, he pleaded for forgiveness, he cried for understanding — and defended his belief in Satanism.

"This is still a free country, isn't it?" he beseeched with tears running down his cheeks. "Isn't freedom of religion what our Revolutionary War heroes paid in blood to protect? Isn't it why the Pilgrims came to Plymouth Rock? And why William Penn founded Philadelphia? My friends, my Christian brothers, don't throw me out just because my beliefs are a little different than yours. Please accept me.

"For your own sakes.

"For your children.

"For America."

What would you do? Well, Tom stared into the TV cameras and began to pray:

"Father," he said. "Am I wrong? Show us truth tonight. Show us plainly. Don't let there be any question in anybody's mind.

"Lord, Your angels fought a mighty battle centuries ago against the forces of Satan. Send them tonight to fight back the forces of confusion and fear. Open our eyes to truth. Your Scriptures tell me that we should not be naive — that Satan is still employing his evil devices against the church to destroy it.

"In the Book of Titus in the Bible, You tell us that if someone comes into our midst and teaches contrary to the Bible — particularly that Satan is good — that we are to gently warn him twice. Then, if he will not be silent, Lord, the Bible tells us that we are to reject him from our fellowship and have nothing more to do with him.

"Well, Lord, give me wisdom now. Is my brother a follower of Satan? If so, am I to ignore Your Holy Bible? Or may I order him to leave us and to go in peace? Amen."

And with that, Tom glanced around at the congregation. You could have heard a pin drop. A sweet, white-haired woman raised her hand. The TV cameras turned to her.

"Yes, Beulah?" said Tom.

"Pastor Tom," she said, standing, her voice strong, her eyes flashing. "My great-great-grandfather fought in the Revolutionary War alongside Ethan Allen and his Green Mountain boys. My grandfather lost his leg in the battle to take Fort Ticonderoga from the Red Coats. I know what it means to fight for freedom."

She turned to the Satanist. "Young man," she said in a grandmotherly way. "If you were to come to my Daughters of the American Revolution meetings and start telling the younger women that Benedict Arnold was misunderstood, that Hitler was really a nice fellow, that the Ayatollah Khomeini actually was doing the best thing for America, well, we would throw you out on your ear!

"And it's no different here in this little church, young man. My forefathers fought and died so that you could worship Satan or Caspar the Ghost or even your own toenails if you wish. But they also fought for their own freedom to worship in peace. That's the real reason why William Penn founded Pennsylvania and why Roger Williams took his people to Rhode Island. So they could worship their God undisturbed by troublemakers. Now, you need to go worship in your own way somewhere else and leave us alone to worship in ours."

It was beautiful.

Even the TV cameramen cheered.

Sneering, the Satanist leered at the old lady. "I happen to know that you have been under psychiatric care for twenty years," he said. "Your own son tried to have you committed."

There was a terrible silence.

Beulah drew herself up to her full five feet, two inches. "Yes," she said. "But by the power of Jesus Christ, I have been delivered. For twenty years, I thought I was a white witch. Now I know the truth. I have broken out of your evil cult. Now, I know why I was half crazy. Jesus has delivered me." She dug in her purse.

"Look here, young man," she said, holding up a voting registration card. "I was certified incapable of taking care of myself five years ago. But by the power of Jesus Christ, my doctor has taken me off of all medication, the court has given me back authority over my own affairs and I've registered to vote once again.

"I am free by the healing power of Jesus Christ. I am free, yes, free indeed. In the name of Jesus Christ."

Wow.

And something interesting happened. Every time that Beulah said the name of Jesus, the troublemaker seemed to cringe. He leered. He sneered. He shrunk back into his seat.

Uttering a curse against God, he spat venom at Tom. "You [obscenity], you don't have the [obscenity] to try to kick me out of here," he hissed. "You [obscenity]! You and your crazy, [obscenity] people are following a [obscenity] dead god."

"No, Jesus Christ lives!" whispered Tom. "And by the power of His holy Name, in the name of Jesus Christ who died for you, I tell you now: 'Go and practice your beliefs elsewhere. In the name of Jesus Christ, go, my friend. And know this, we love you.'"

The Satanist stalked out, spitting insults and curses

under his breath, threatening legal action. But his own lawyer just sat on his hands, waiting for Tom to do or say something that would allow them to sue.

Operating in the Lord's wisdom and the power of the Holy Spirit, Tom didn't do anything foolish.

He hated everything the witches stood for — despised it. But he had to look past all the antics and insults and see hurting people that Jesus Christ loves.

And Tom had to love them with pure Jesus love.

What followed were several very difficult years.

At least two more infiltrators were sent to cause all sorts of havoc.

One was a "hurt lamb," bruised, needing compassion. After they found housing for her, provided food, gave her money out of their own pockets and did all kinds of things to help her, she started to make subtle accusations regarding Tom, that he had made sexual advances towards her.

However, the first person she tried it with rebuked her boldly! Tom's church members were becoming a small army of spiritual warriors who now knew how to identify evil and biblically deal with it.

The third infiltrator was converted.

Genuinely.

Tearfully, beautifully, honestly — she came to Jesus after weeks of putting on an act. It turned out she, too, was a second-generation Satanist.

What glorious victory!

But the assault didn't let up.

5

Betrayed
by Friends

Each day Tom and Leisha didn't know what they would face. Leisha kept the door to the office locked and bolted because they'd had so many threats on their lives. There were constant messages left on their answering machine, threats that they would be killed if they didn't get out of town.

The Satanists wanted their ex-members back!

At any cost.

They would follow the former infiltrator to services, threatening her life. She would arrive home to find life-threatening messages written in blood on her door.

One evening Tom was coming out of a service when a woman appeared from nowhere. She began hissing and cursing him.

With full confidence he pointed his finger into her face and told her, "I rebuke you in the name of Jesus and I command you to get out of here!"

She turned and fled!

You see, the devil is always trying to get you off guard. We must be ready, instantly, in season and out.

Tom had taken the kids of the church outside to a nearby park. A demon-possessed man approached and tried to interrupt.

"Thus sayeth he that believeth and seeth, yea, verily," the man uttered mystically, "Woe to you who cometh to me and does not enter unto it. Behold, I say that our begotten prayers are not beholden to this generation: judge not." On and on, he yammered all kinds of jumbled-up mess that sounded holy enough — but meant nothing.

Again, Tom ordered him away in the name of Jesus. Muttering, the man left.

Tom was learning: You must not allow the devil an inch! Be strong, forceful, defending the turf God has given you.

And you have to do it in your personal life, too.

You have to be blameless.

Because Satan is the accuser.

His accusations will hurt. You will be misunderstood, too. Even fellow Christians began criticizing Tom as being "unchristian," "unloving" and "heartless" to the poor, dear Satanists breaking out his car windows, vandalizing his church and terrorizing his flock.

"We're supposed to turn the other cheek," fellow pastors cautioned Tom.

They did not understand that day in and day out, in the power of the Lord, he did just that, turning the other cheek, loving those who utterly despised him and wanted to see him dead, his wife destitute and his son bowing down to Lucifer.

Do we always turn the other cheek?

Brother, you better not turn your other cheek to the devil. He may just blow it off for you! We are allowed to fight back! But we have to do it in God's power—just like I've been trying to show you in these examples of Island Pond and Tom and Leisha.

Yes, we can fight back. In His time.

Under His guidance.

In His strength.

We are not required to love evil, nor the acts of evil. You can still have a compassionate love for the sinner— that person caught up in deception, but you'd better be tough in the face of evil — while loving the person and attempting to lead them to salvation.

Perhaps the hardest test that Tom and Leisha endured was when Satan began turning fellow Christians against them.

They were "too aggressive," fellow pastors chided: stop all this confrontation, rest in the Lord. So many times, Tom was moved to tears of anger. His ministry was growing in its effectiveness — reaching adults and kids deep into drug trafficking, pornographic horror films, sadism, madness, murder and blood sacrifice.

Addicts, spiritualists, adulterers, voodoo dabblers, thieves, witches, con-artists — all were coming to Jesus and giving up their dance with the darkness ... as well as their all-too-common, greedy exploitation of earnest searchers for truth.

Marriages were being restored, finances were turning around and there were baptisms every week.

Yet since attendance at their church hovered right around fifty, fellow preachers began to tell Tom and Leisha that they were "failing."

That was harder to take than the blood-scrawled

threats on the windows! At least with the enemy you can understand it and comprehend it because that's what you expect. But when your heart is torn in two, the hardest thing to receive is a hurt inflicted by a well-meaning friend.

Tom and Leisha would attend pastors' functions only to come away hurt and bruised. "Tom, you can't build a viable church with those type of people," fellow pastors advised. "You need young, upwardly mobile professionals to build a church today. You need people with two incomes who will donate generously."

The young couple had to guard themselves from bitterness. The devil was using the brethren to beat them down.

And it was working.

Finally, one large church withdrew its financial support, following a board meeting in which Tom and Leisha were roundly criticized — and ripped apart emotionally.

But in the car on the way home, they just agreed together in Jesus' name that they would make it. God was their source — not the big-city church that no longer understood.

Sometimes, you will be alone in your fight.

That's when we must be so careful! You must have good fellowship with believers who will bear your burdens with you — as you bear theirs! You need intercessors, people who will pray for you. Ask the Lord to send them to you.

But don't — let me repeat — don't try to be the Lone Ranger. You cannot fight and win alone.

You see, the devil loves to play games with your mind. If he can get you to believe somehow he has a hold over you, he's got you.

So, you need good fellowship.

And you need to stay in the Word.

I'm talking about daily Bible study and a good, private quiet time with the Lord. The Bible talks about renewing our minds. We must daily renew our minds in good, solid time with our Creator.

The second bomb threat was called into the sheriff's dispatcher. A deputy drove out to Mannatu Crossing and strolled into the church office with an attitude of "Okay, what did you guys do this time?" He was crass and sarcastic — just going through the motions of responding to a bomb threat "by the book."

"The first time you don't take one of these guys seriously, deputy, will be the time you regret," Leisha told him with great seriousness.

He looked at her and he said, "What is it about your church that seems to draw this kind of activity?"

Leisha thought for a moment and then asked the Father to quickly give her a wise answer this man would understand. "Well, it could be a number of things," she said, "It could be that they're mad that they can't take advantage of us and that we don't act like the state department of social services. Or it could be that they just can't stand the Spirit of God."

He pondered that for a moment and then solemnly left. Back at the sheriff's office, they traced the threatening call to a phone booth on a street corner. They brought a man into custody and informed Tom and Leisha that they needed to come in and identify him and press charges.

Tom went down to the station first. The man was covered in black and had an upside-down cross tattooed in the middle of his forehead. He had all sorts of occult symbols, from jacket patches to jewelry to tattoos. Tom squared off face-to-face with him, he in his cell and Tom through the bars said, "Hey, what do you have against churches?"

"Nothing, man, nothing!"

"What's that on your forehead?"

"Nothing, man, nothing!" as he pushed his hair down to cover it.

Tom had never seen him before, but discerned he was a young occultist, probably going through the hazing process — trying to get into a group. His requirement was probably to hit a church and go as far as he could to destroy it.

The following Sunday evening, Tom and Leisha were at the church setting up for the service. Leisha was in the office when she heard loud screaming. She quickly phoned the sheriff, then ran over to the sanctuary to find a woman attacking Tom.

She was pointing her finger in his face cursing him, physically striking out at him. Tom stood there calmly rebuking her in the name and blood of Jesus. He was slowly backing her towards the doorway when the sheriff arrived. She quickly ran out and the deputies followed.

It took three large county deputies to handcuff her and haul her away. Tom pressed trespassing charges. In her fear of appearing in court, she waited outside the church one evening on the sidewalk and begged him not to press charges. She asked forgiveness and Tom dropped the matter.

They never saw her again after that.

One of the policemen who arrested her asked Tom if he'd heard about Josephine.

"No, I'm not sure who you mean." Tom said. "Well, I

was called out last week on that bomb threat character, you know the one you came in to identify."

"Right, the occultist with the upside down cross tattoo in his forehead." Tom stated.

"Turns out our Joe turned out to be a Josephine! For real, I was assigned to take the pictures of his tattoos and when he took off his shirt, he was a she!"

It is a common thing for an occultist, especially those in Satanism to be confused over their sexuality.

Things quieted down after a time ... and Tom and Leisha supposed the enemy had learned he was in a losing battle. But just when you think you're on top, watch out. The devil is a sneak and a liar and will attempt anything. Don't put anything past him. Don't ever think you've arrived, don't ever get comfortable.

This story is longer than we have room to tell here. But it is a tale of continuing victory.

The church had a successful fund-raising drive and soon moved to a larger facility. It happens to be located a little outside of the wide spot in the road that is Mannatu Crossing.

Tom sees that as God's providence.

And mercy.

The fine building that He provided is closer to town. And the church is becoming a real church — with ordinary people mingling with the ex-Buddhists, former witches, ex-Satan worshipers, former fortune-tellers and ex-fire walkers.

Tom sees that as a sign of success. His flock is not just a bunch of ex-rejects. They're fitting in. They're no longer wild-eyed former crazies that scare off everyday folks.

The battle continues.

But it no longer consumes Tom and Leisha to the point

that they cannot focus on mundane, necessary church stuff such as what Vacation Bible School program to use next summer or whether to have Family Night on Wednesdays or Thursdays.

This is a story of victory.

But the battle goes on.

Pray for Tom and Leisha. They are a wonderful pair. They are battle-toughened and a little battle weary.

But they know how to fight back.

And win.

6

Fighting with Gratitude

It's difficult to give thanks in the middle of a sex scandal. How do you give thanks amid humiliating disaster — as you watch your dreams go up in flames?

Yet, Paul the apostle writes, "In all things, give thanks."

So, how?

A large church in California was the life dream of a longtime friend of mine, one of the better-known author-evangelists in America. He had founded the congregation and nurtured it through good and bad times.

Now, in his declining years, the ministry was something of which to be truly proud. It had been featured in Christian magazines and cited in at least one book as a model for all of us to emulate.

I mean, it had a nationally recognized children's outreach led by a husband and wife who were packaging their curriculum for a publishing company's new Sunday school program.

It had an outstanding Christian school, an excellent
orchestra that played on a number of praise albums, an
effective ministry to substance abusers that had been
featured as the cover story of a national magazine, a
strong network of home Bible study fellowships, an
international tape ministry, a traveling mime troupe, a
puppet team, and an award-winning program for retirees.

The music ministry was headed by a nationally-
acclaimed worship leader who led week-long seminars
nationwide. He shared song-leading duties with three
globe-trotting Christian recording artists who utilized
this California church as their national base of operations.

But as happens in even the best of churches, dissent
and division emerged when the senior pastor brought in
a fireball of an assistant pastor, whom we'll call Alan.
The senior pastor then hit the road to accept a long list
of standing invitations to appear on TV and speak in
some of the biggest churches in America.

Alan was a fine speaker and an excellent one-on-one
counselor. He genuinely cared about his new flock.

The congregation fell in love with him.

In fact, in the absence of their senior pastor, the
congregation just naturally turned to Alan for weddings,
funerals, baptisms and spiritual guidance. In particular,
Alan developed a large following when he started a
Thursday afternoon ladies' Bible study. The women of
the church loved him.

Amid all the acclaim, within eighteen months, Alan
found himself growing uncomfortable. He grew resentful in his secondary role — playing second banana to the
famous senior pastor and best-selling author. Whenever
the senior pastor's travels brought him home, the old
man retook his old pulpit — joyously reporting all his

adventures, recounting experiences on Christian TV, excitedly telling of meeting Christian celebrities.

Alan became covetous.

After all, the people now looked to Alan. Day in and day out, he cared for these hurting people — this flock of 4,500 — abandoned by their wandering TV star.

It was Alan who put in 60 hours a week overseeing the pastoral staff of fifteen, preaching in the three morning services, nurturing new leadership, leading the Sunday evening prayer service, developing a new board of deacons, as well as watching over the music, retirees, drug-addiction and children's ministries. Frequently, Alan attended five church meetings a day — dropping in, noting that all was well, offering guidance and moving on. And Alan led an increasingly popular Thursday night men's fellowship.

But Alan grew bitter that he was not the top gun.

Why didn't the senior pastor see that it was time to move on? The church was now Alan's. Why didn't the old man just retire and write books?

Alan lusted for the pulpit whenever the senior pastor returned home. Enviously, he writhed in his seat as the old man shared his experiences.

Who did the old goat think he was? He thought he could just pop in and grab the spotlight whenever he wished. And on TV talk shows, he was not above taking credit for all of Alan's hard work as he talked glowingly of the growth his church back home was experiencing.

Great anger grew within the assistant pastor. His inner circle of friends began whispering in his ear that it was time to lead a palace coup — to topple the old man — to force the graying author into retirement.

Quietly Alan inventoried his assets: Alan knew the

music department was with him — grateful for the new
freedom and latitude Alan had permitted in the old
man's absence. The deacons were with him. The ladies
Bible study was certainly with him. The children's
pastor was with him, thrilled with Alan's allowing him
to get rid of the old Sunday school superintendent and
initiate an even more experimental kids' program. And
the men of the Thursday night fellowship would follow
him anywhere.

Sure of his political position, Alan gave the church
trustees an ultimatum: Can the old man — or else.

Calling the senior pastor home for an emergency
meeting, the trustees met with him and Alan, who
proclaimed that there was no room here for two bulls.
One would have to be put out to pasture.

Sadly, the trustees agreed.

They dismissed Alan.

In disbelief, he spat his defiance: "I'll empty this
building — I'll turn it into a garage," he threatened. "I'll
start my own church in the richest part of town and take
all your big contributors — your faithful tithers — with
me. I'll take your kids' program and all their yuppie
parents — and I'll take the choir and the orchestra.
They're with me. You'll have nothing. You're going to sit
in an empty auditorium, staring at each other, unable to
pay the mortgage."

Go with our blessing, said the trustees.

With a pale face, the senior pastor watched in silence.
That evening, he began cancelling his speaking en-
gagements. He had erred, he knew. While he was off
becoming a big shot, Satan was having a heyday.

How can this be, he thought. His heart was broken.
How he loved and trusted Alan. The pain was intense.

He wondered how he could continue.

The church was a shambles. Whether they realized it or not, the members had been given a choice of allegiance: to Alan or their famous senior pastor. What about Jesus?

Further, it had been the senior pastor's dream for years that his fellowship would plant small congregations all over town. He had never planned to lead a megachurch, such as his had become. How had he allowed this disaster to happen?

That Sunday, Alan was permitted to announce from the pulpit the formation of a new church in the southern, more affluent part of town. The senior pastor solemnly joined him at the microphone and quietly gave his blessing to the "new sister church" — and even pledged financial support to get the work underway.

The new church had its first service the following week — with 1,500 crowding a high school gymnasium fifteen miles south. The children's program hit the ground running — with teachers and helpers lined up and ready to teach in both services and Sunday school.

It was a glorious Sunday:

Two recording artists led singing from banks of keyboards at either side of the platform. Virtually the entire orchestra was there, too, following their worship leader, who knew he would have absolute freedom to try anything — since Alan needed him to make this new church work.

At the door, worshipers were given colored handkerchiefs to wave during the song service. A group of children danced up and down the aisles, twirling colorful ribbons in the air. White-robed dancers whirled around the platform. High school boys in satin shirts held high beautiful banners proclaiming God's greatness.

In front of the choir, a bank of women did synchro-

nized sign-language interpretation — like holy hula
dancers. A couple of ballet dancers pirouetted across the
platform. Various singers stood on the edges of the stage,
caressing microphones and drawing the crowd into ec-
static choruses.

It was ... memorable.

Back at the old church, things were considerably more
quiet. The senior pastor spoke to about 2,000 stalwarts
and led them in thanksgiving and prayer for the new
church.

"God is in control," proclaimed the old man — saddened
by the small crowd, and knowing that many had stayed
home from either service, disgusted by the ugliness and
dissension.

For more than a year, the older church helped support
the new one.

But the senior pastor could not help but be disturbed
by the growing effort by Alan and his staff to try to do
everything bigger and better than the older church.
Alan's attitude seemed to be: "Fire me, will you? Well, I'll
show you how to hold church."

Then, one morning, the senior pastor heard a knock on
the back door of his home. It was a very humbled Alan.

"Pastor, I need to talk to you," Alan said, looking
downward. "This morning, my deacons fired me. Pastor,
I was caught in adultery. I have been having an affair
with the worship leader's wife.

"It started off as an innocent friendship," he confessed.
"Then things between us started getting more complicated and before I knew what was happening, I was
lusting for her body. I knew it was wrong, but twice we
succumbed and had sexual relations. I swear it was only
twice.

"So, I'm human! So, I stumbled!" he wept. "I'm not Jesus Christ! Our affair cooled substantially in the last 60 days. So, how could they fire me for something I've stopped doing? How could this happen? I was only trying to spread the gospel and lead hundreds of people to Jesus."

"Praise God," whispered the senior pastor as he prayed with Alan. "Lord, You are in control. You are master. You know what You are doing. Thank You for Your goodness to us."

In the next days, the community was rocked by the scandal as the news grew worse:

• The treasurer of the church began revealing financial improprieties that Alan had demanded: that the church pay all his utilities, credit cards and home mortgage as church expenses, that Alan had frequently made cash withdrawals which he ordered labeled as anything but salary, and that Alan had insisted that his reported income to the IRS be substantially less than what he'd actually been paid. Worse, Alan had recently begun taking wads of loose cash when the Sunday offering was brought in. That income was never reported as required by law.

• Then the young man who led the dance troupe confessed to his wife that he had been involved in homosexual liaisons with one of the recording artists who sang and played the piano most Sundays. Further, he declared, he wanted a divorce so he could to move to San Francisco with his friend — who had left his wife a year before.

• Next, one of the deacons, who had put together a mutual fund investment program for church members, disappeared with all the money.

• Then, a college coed who had been staying with the choir director's family confessed to allowing her boyfriend to videotape simulated sexual acts with her and a number of boys in the high school youth group — for a college film project.

• And the daughter of the children's pastor was expelled from her school for brutalizing a younger girl in the gym locker room with a pellet gun.

One by one, everyone on staff was scandalized—either by a spouse or by a member of their household or by their own misbehavior.

The local newspapers bannered the scandal across front pages: "Sex, lies and videotape … and a fleeced flock," read one snide headline, parroting the title of an Academy Award-winning sex movie.

That Sunday, the significantly humbled church — with a crowd of less than 350 — met in their high school gym fifteen miles south of the old church. One of the deacons played the piano. The orchestra was sparse. The choir was, too. All the pastors and worship leaders were gone. A local policeman who was an usher nervously gave a very simple sermon on having an attitude of gratitude.

"We don't know why some things happen," he said, taking his text from the Book of Job. "But I know that God is here. He loves you and me. And He is in control."

A spontaneous altar call lasted more than 45 minutes — with virtually everybody in attendance down at the platform, weeping, and thanking the Lord for whatever He was doing.

The new church survived.

Today it is maybe half as big as it was at first. But it is a solid congregation — in good fellowship with its sister church fifteen miles north. The worship service is joyous. The new pastor has been given incredible freedom by his Bible-believing deacons to follow the Spirit's leading.

Alan has accepted a public relations job with a local electronics corporation. One worship leader has moved his family to Nashville. The two in the homosexual tryst are submitting to Christian counseling although neither has yet returned to his wife.

What was the key to survival in the midst of this horrible Peyton Place scandal of all church scandals?

Years of teaching that we must always have an attitude of gratitude.

That we must give thanks in all things.

Another key element was the prayerful intercession of the old pastor — thanking the Lord for remaining in control amid the mess.

A major factor was his earlier years of instilling in his flock longtime habits of thanking God for His constant protection, His provision and His leading no matter how bad things may look in human eyes.

I know it's hard to have an attitude of gratitude if someone has caused you a deep, undeserved hurt. Believe it or not, it's even worse if you deserve it — like Alan — if you know you are guilty of terrible things and completely undeserving of the Lord's mercy.

Yet, that's a time when God can do great things.

When we come to the Lord, our hands dirty or even bloody from our sin — humbly asking His forgiveness and thanking Him for His mercy — He can be so gracious.

He can be so loving.

Guilty of lying, cheating, you name it, you or I can rock

in Jesus' arms and know that He still loves us — just liked He loved Zacchaeus, the crooked tax collector, and the prostitutes and the people who flocked after Him expecting free, miraculous meals.

We are still going to have to pay the earthly consequences of our sin.

But, if we come to Him humbly, sorry for our rotten behavior, asking for His help to be strong enough to say "No!" next time, He accepts us home — the lost, black sheep that we are.

I have a friend, Marc, who got caught up in what was very close to being a scam. Marc hired a "super salesman" and paid him $152,000 in extravagant commissions over 27 months. The salesman promised Marc's customers far more than he could deliver, gave away products at below cost, and severely oversold my friend's company's ability to produce.

I, myself, paid $4,100 for copies of a videotape that I provide through my ministry.

I never did get my tapes — which, I'll have to tell you, really caused a nasty rift between me and my friend Marc. I felt seriously betrayed, particularly as the bigger picture emerged.

When everything crashed, Marc was left holding the bag for hundreds of thousands of dollars in orders that his insolvent company was never going to be able to produce.

Although he felt he had done nothing wrong — in fact Marc had virtually killed himself trying to pull the company through — the ultimate responsibility lay with him.

Marc had not kept his hand in every deal.

He had not carefully watched every penny spent. And

as clients became increasingly anxious, Marc had promised them the moon — determined that he was going to make it all come out okay.

And so, when the company collapsed, it was Marc's fault. He had let it happen.

He had not worked hard enough. He had not asked the Lord to do whatever needed to be done in his life to rescue this mess.

It was Marc's fault.

He owed everybody in the country money. He owed people in foreign countries. He owed suppliers. He owed manufacturers. He owed friends.

Marc even owed himself money.

While he was paying the salesman $152,000 to give his company away, Marc paid himself and his wife only about $30,000 a year — and worked 90-hour weeks.

But nevertheless, the mess was his fault.

As the disaster deepened, as the burden of guilt grew heavier on my friend's shoulders, as everything caved in around his head, guess where Marc found hope — and sanity?

In an attitude of gratitude.

He looked to his only Source.

Marc thanked the Lord for the incredible things that God did to keep my friend from going crazy, losing his family or denouncing his faith.

An attitude of gratitude helped Marc fight back and win — although he lost his company and it may take years for him to regain his reputation.

The fact remained that the fiasco was his fault.

He had to move his wife and four kids 1,400 miles in a rental truck to take a job far from home.

But my friend saw and knew that a loving, wonderful

Lord was the reason his wife was not losing her mind over the disaster. He realized that a gracious Lord would allow his large family to live on the substantially reduced salary — and that God would provide for his needs and even his wants.

He knew it was the Lord who gave his kids peace and even excitement about leaving their home near the beach and helped them to adjust quickly and happily to their new home, their new school and their new friends.

And it was the Lord that gave Marc a challenging new job where he could work with generous and godly people, use his talents to further the Kingdom and fit into a community that did not care about the horrible failure that he had left behind.

An attitude of gratitude.

It was Marc's key to survival.

An attitude of gratitude is one of the most effective ways God gives you and me to fight back in His strength. Despite the great worries that may be devouring your faith, keep your eyes on Jesus — and keep thanking Him for His great goodness to you.

See and know that He is in control — no matter how bad things are falling apart.

Angry, bitter and resentful, Alan never gave up his faith. Why? Because his old rival, the senior pastor, helped him see it was God who kept Alan's wife from divorcing him in mid-scandal. It was the Lord who found Alan a good-paying job.

And it was the Lord who still loved His fallen child.

And Alan saw it.

He knew who his deliverer was.

And he was grateful.

Remember that things looked terrible to the Israelites

as they wandered around the Sinai desert, grumbling about having to eat manna.

But God was in control back then.

Just as he is now.

Your generous, loving God had a wonderful Promised Land waiting for those freed slaves. He had incredible, impossible military victories planned — preposterous triumphs against ridiculous odds. I mean, these folks marched around fortified cities, tooted horns, shouted and just watched as city walls toppled over!

He gave them the victory, but they had to use the power and might of the Holy Spirit to conquer, as we must today.

They were involved.

They were given battle plans. Under God's guidance, Joshua ordered them to advance! They had to obey the word of their heavenly commander — and His human generals — or it wouldn't work.

They obeyed and entered the cities victorious.

People, today we also can be victors, but we must follow the battle plan. The Word of God.

We must listen to our commander.

Then, always, the enemy will suffer defeat.

7

The Weapon of Forgiveness

What allowed the older, senior pastor to be so kind and loving to Alan, the irksome young usurper? I'll tell you right now that the old man is no angel. He and I have been close friends for years and the man has many faults.

In his early years of ministry, he was involved in two terrible affairs with women in his church. He has a history of neglecting people he has promised to nurture.

He has an unfortunate fascination with the human politics that can pit ambitious brother against brother within a large church. And he has been a bit of a dynasty builder in his ministry — promoting his own children into key positions in the church whether or not they merited it.

But he has been forgiven so many times for his own foul-ups that he knows the need that you and I have to forgive those who do us dirt. We just can't carry around the heartache, the resentment, the anger.

He knows that the Lord will make something wonderful out of what the devil would like to be utter devastation — if we will forgive.

Forgive?

Forgiving some jerk who took advantage of you can heal enormous hurts. And it does not make you a doormat. Forgiving is not a holy, righteous, sacrificial obligation to be nice to some wretch who's been vicious to you. It's not a "Please Kick Me Again" sign taped onto your back when you kneel at the altar.

Forgiving is the opportunity God gives you and me to stop hurting.

Don Francisco, the Christian singer, has a love song on one of his albums that says a lot to a world trying to figure out just what love is.

"Love is not a feeling," he sings. "It's an act of the will."

And so is forgiveness.

Rarely is forgiveness the natural, instinctive thing to do. No, the automatic response is to go punch your offender in the nose.

But forgiveness allows you to put the matter to rest.

How can you forgive somebody who has done terrible things to you? Ask their forgiveness.

A friend of mine hung onto enormous hurt for years when the Christian owner of a large company seemingly wronged him.

My friend nursed a grudge for a long time.

But then, one day, he knew he had to forgive his old boss.

He made an appointment.

They met face-to-face for the first time since the owner had robbed him of his Christmas bonus, removed him from his prestigious position and caused him to have to take a demeaning job with a smaller company.

"I just wanted you to know that I'm sorry that I let you down," said my friend.

His former boss, who may have been expecting a lawsuit, blinked in surprise. "That's right," he sputtered. "You let me down." Then the man stood. He held out his hand in friendship. "But I forgive you."

Calmly, my friend smiled.

And he knew it was all over.

He was free to love his old boss.

To love him.

To pray for him.

Because he wasn't mad any longer.

He had forgiven the guy.

He had elected to forgive instead of nurturing anger and resentment.

When I counsel people with marital problems, it's easy to detect the one who has made the decision to terminate the marriage. They've quit trying to forgive.

The decision to forgive a person involves a commitment. It requires an investment of energy.

The decision to forgive isn't a passive act.

Indeed, when you find a marriage that has lasted 25, 50 or even 75 years, you'll discover that the husband and wife exercised a conscious will to continue forgiving each other.

It's never easy to ask for forgiveness when you behave toward your spouse like an absolute jerk.

But it works.

Let me tell you something else about a forgiving attitude. It will help you endure the worst.

Bitsy was a cute, wonderful daughter of missionaries — a sincere, devout Christian who made straight-A's, spoke three languages fluently and was delighted when she won a scholarship to one of America's better Christian universities.

But in her sophomore year, she gave in just once to the tender caresses of a boy she didn't really love at all.

And once was all it took.

Not only did she lose the virginity she had been saving for her eventual husband, but she became pregnant.

No, it wasn't fair.

All around her, on TV, in the movies, even at school, other girls were blatantly promiscuous — and seemingly bore no consequences.

But Bitsy, in her one, single act of passion, got pregnant.

She dropped out of school and was taken in by friends of her family. She went on welfare — since she could not work in the latter months of her pregnancy nor immediately afterward.

Eventually, she got a job as a payables clerk at a janitorial service. The pay was enough that she could pay her friends room and board — and day care for little Mitchell.

But her dreams evaporated.

College was over.

Her dreams of becoming a psychologist were finished.

No nice Christian guy was going to date her — she was the adulteress, an unwed teen, a fallen hussy with loose morals.

But instead of letting bitterness overtake her, Bitsy consciously worked on an attitude of gratitude — and forgiveness.

For, you see, Bitsy was angry at God.

Furious.

How had He allowed this disaster?

Other girls were blatantly promiscuous, and bragged of their collection of conquests. Her own little brother had really gotten into the Latin American macho spirit and constantly was seducing innocent young girls.

But nothing happened to him. So, why did all the consequences fall on Bitsy — the good girl with straight-As and a scholarship to a prestigious school?

Bitsy was bitter.

She was hurt.

She felt abandoned.

But then she realized that God was there. He was taking care of her.

• After all, Mitchell was a beautiful, intelligent baby and an absolute delight;

• God had provided her with good, supportive friends willing to take her into their home as long as she needed a place to stay;

• Her dad did not turn his back on her as she had feared — no, instead, he sent Mitchie all sorts of baby clothes and toys from South America, along with funny letters addressed to both Bitsy and the boy;

• And she was gradually putting aside savings. There was a real chance that someday she would be able to start back to college.

Tearfully, on her knees, Bitsy asked forgiveness for blaming God.

And she forgave the boy who had seduced her.

She began looking at everything in a different light — of forgiveness instead of bitterness and gratitude instead of resentment.

Instead of anxiously looking for a husband or praying desperately that the Lord would send the right man to rescue her, Bitsy realized that it was entirely possible that the rest of her life might be spent single — just her and little Mitch. She looked to the Lord as the priest of her house and the father of her fatherless little guy.

And she thanked the Lord for giving her a good job with nice people — and with a company where she had excellent potential for advancement.

Relaxing in God's goodness, nurturing an attitude of praising the Lord for everything, Bitsy settled back into her new life. She got her own apartment and enrolled in night school.

As she thanked God for His goodness.

Today she is the happily married wife of a hard-working airline mechanic named Derek — who makes good money and hopes to someday be a missionary. They have three darling kids, including nine-year-old Mitch, who her husband has adopted and given his name.

"I never thought I would find anybody who would want me," Bitsy told me. "But God is so good. Derek and Mitchie even look alike. Nobody knows our past. It's just our private little secret.

"And I'll tell you what got me through it all:

"When I forgave."

Forgiveness takes the wind out of Satan's sails. His evil devices turn into an ebb-tide of his power. We throw his foul plans back into his face. Forgiveness frees us from the bondage the devil has planned for us.

Unforgiveness only makes us his slave.

He has been defeated and we have the power given us by God to keep him there.

And forgiveness is one of our weapons!

8

Winning
Against Child Abuse

The dark-eyed little girls had a terrible secret.

The four-year-old and her seven-year-old sister did not know how horrible a secret it truly was.

But their new "grandpa" saw their terror.

And it broke his heart.

He was a Christian physician. He and his wife have for years taken in people in distress — turning their nice home into a sort of Holy Ghost hospital.

One Sunday night, a distraught woman had answered the altar call at their church. Melissa wept with the pastor as she shared a horrible story.

As a child, she had been repeatedly molested by her grandfather — as had her little sisters.

Melissa had married, escaping from the horror.

But her husband had turned out to be violently abusive. And now, she had to admit what she had been denying to herself — the horrible truth that he had been abusing their little daughters sexually for years.

She had tried to close her eyes to it — disbelieving that this horror from her childhood had returned.

Then her vicious husband had become convinced there was big money to be made in child pornography — and had ordered Melissa to help him try videotaping the girls doing degrading things that Melissa could barely describe to strangers.

After a violent argument during which he knocked out Melissa's front teeth, she fled with her girls, taking refuge 500 miles from home at a shelter for battered women. Now, at Sunday evening church, she had come to the Lord ...

In terrible distress.

Searching for answers.

Needing hope.

On the first night in their new home, the little sisters fearfully looked up at their new "grandpa" as he came in to kiss them good-night.

Their eyes glazing in terrible fear, both lifted their little nighties and mechanically spread their trembling legs.

The Christian physician wept as he gently covered them with a fluffy blanket. Both little girls looked confused. They did not understand.

They thought he had come in to have sex.

What horror these tiny, innocent children had endured! Molestation had been a commonplace, daily occurrence in their lives.

They were ages four and seven. A pre-schooler and a second grader. Naturally pretty. Dark-eyed. But filled with anger, suspicion, terror and defeat. Accusations radiated from their eyes. Pain filled their trembling faces. Fear raged in their little hearts.

But brutality had taught them submission.

So, they silently accepted their nightmare.

And they assumed this man would be like the only other one they had ever known.

Sexual abuse of children is such a shocking subject — one that many people would much rather ignore.

But the statistics are staggering:

• One out of every three girls is sexually abused before she reaches the age of eighteen.

• One out of every five boys is molested before he reaches legal age.

• Ninety percent of the offenders are known to their victims.

• Fifty-six percent of offenders are under the age of eighteen.

• Five percent of offenders are psychotic.

• Twenty to thirty percent do not have the ability to care about other people because their personality development was arrested at an early stage.

• If not stopped, some molesters will hurt 1,500 children in a lifetime. These are what are called "fixated" offenders, dangerous perverts who have not developed emotionally because of a traumatic experience, often their own molestation as a child. Many get jobs that will permit them access to the kids on whom they are fixated, working as school janitors, playground workers, teachers, Scout leaders and camp counselors.

• A much larger percentage — called "regressed" offenders — molest kids they know, often as the result of an adult crisis in their life.

• Women molest children as much as men — but are much less likely to get reported. Indeed, increasingly, the woman who seduces a young boy is lionized in movies and books as doing the child a favor—when, in fact, most of the boys are severely traumatized from the seduction.

Some perpetrators start out with what may seem to be "victimless" sexual sin — maybe pornography, starting with girlie magazines, escalating to the bizarre, the sado-masochistic and child pornography.

What can be done to fight back?

• Get the child away from the molester. End all contact.

• Report the incident to police or social services. Failing to do so will leave the child in serious danger. The molester is in bondage to sin and will do it again and again unless apprehended.

• Get counseling for the offender. Most who receive help do not do it again.

• Fight the things that spur this sort of activity: pornography, sex films, dirty books, filth on TV and so forth;

• Learn where the road that leads to sin starts.

• Take the whole issue out of the closet and deal with it honestly — do not hide it in shame.

• Pray. Seek the wisdom and guidance of the Holy Spirit.

The Bible says we must walk in the light.

That means we do not focus in on the horrible. We cannot become consumed with this disgusting, perhaps provocative problem and take our eyes off of the joy, hope and provision of Jesus Christ.

But it also means we cannot hide sin. What keeps so many people in bondage to this sin, is a great conspiracy of silence. The subject is too terrible to discuss.

If an incident occurs, it is hushed up.

The assistant pastor's teen-age son was accused of

abusing a small child at a church in which I've preached. Here's what happened.

The child's mother was a shy, divorced mother of three with very little self-confidence. She came to the church's volunteer Sunday school superintendent with this terrible story.

She had come home one night to find her eight-year-old daughter performing oral sex on the baby-sitter, a sixteen-year-old boy who lived down the street. The little girl's older brother and sister were in their rooms, ignoring what was going on.

Hysterical, the mother demanded to know why the older children were pretending nothing was happening.

"I didn't want to look at it," shrugged the ten-year-old brother defensively. "Jeannie was being naughty and I didn't want to watch it. She does it all the time to him. He wanted her to do it to me, but I wouldn't let her. She's disgusting. She's so bad. I hate her."

"I told her not to do it," wept little Jeannie's seventh-grader sister. "But he said if I told anybody, he'd tell the ninth grade boys at school that I would do it, too. And I won't."

The mother had marched the sixteen-year-old baby-sitter home, where his parents became angry — but at her not their son. They said that if little Jeannie's mother reported this to authorities, she would lose her children.

"You'd better keep this quiet if you want to keep your brats," sneered the sixteen-year-old's father. "The day you report this, they'll grab your kids into a foster home so fast it'll make your head spin. You should have been at home, not off doing your thing."

"Doing her thing" had been working — making a

living.

Shaken, the mother went home and talked with her little Jeannie — who laughingly acted as if the whole thing was just a fun game. It was exciting. It got her enormous attention from the boy.

Then, she said that she also did it every Sunday with Matt, the fourteen-year-old son of the assistant pastor, during junior church.

Weeping, the mother called the Sunday school superintendent. He listened grimly — shocked and stunned.

This family and certainly little Jeannie needed help — and quickly. She was too young to understand how serious her "little game" really was. Without real help, she was going to take some deep and terrible scars with her into adolescence and adulthood — as the seriousness of what had happened sank in.

He felt that the sixteen-year-old baby-sitter needed to be reported to authorities since he had done the actual molestation — coaching the little girl to perform oral sex.

The Sunday school superintendent had a different view of young Matt, the assistant pastor's son — also guilty of a taking advantage of this little girl. He knew Matt needed somebody to talk with him — lovingly, understandingly, sternly and with warnings.

And the older kids of little Jeannie's family needed ministry.

But the superintendent knew that this sort of thing can be a real field day for Satan. This topic is so shocking and hush-hush that mere whispers of such a scandal can rock a community and close down a church.

So, real wisdom was going to be needed. If the newspaper found out, Jeannie's and Matt's young reputations could be ruined. The church could be branded as a place of perversion and an unsafe place for children.

The Sunday school superintendent knew that he, too, might be liable legally. Although he was a volunteer, he was responsible for the well-being of all the kids in Sunday school. After all, he had somehow not done whatever was necessary to keep an eight-year-old girl who liked to perform oral sex from connecting with a fourteen-year-old perfectly willing to let her do so.

The Sunday school superintendent's head began to spin as he realized the overpowering, critical nature of this nightmare.

He called up the assistant pastor.

"Darrell," he said. "We have a major problem. A little girl in the church has been molested by a sixteen-year-old boy in her neighborhood. The mother is scared to report it — she says that she doesn't want to lose her daughter or have her put into a foster home."

"The law in this state is clear," answered the assistant pastor. "If you know about an unprosecuted crime, you have to report it or else you become an accessory after the fact. You need to go with the child's parents to city hall and make a police report. Tell the parents that if they report the incident immediately, the police will treat it like a rape or any other assault."

"Look, it's a little more complicated," said the Sunday school superintendent. "The little girl also says that your son, Matt, molested her, too. During junior church — in the pastor's private bathroom."

There was a stunned silence.

"Have you told anybody else about this?" asked the assistant pastor.

"No."

"Do you realize how much trouble this could cause?"

"I certainly do, Darrell. That's why I called you first."

"What were you doing counseling this woman?" demanded the assistant pastor. "You aren't on the pastoral staff. You don't have any background to give professional counseling. You aren't qualified. Where did you think you had the right to give spiritual guidance?"

"What do you mean?" asked the Sunday school superintendent.

"You're out of line. You have overstepped your authority," raged the assistant pastor. "You can't start handing out spiritual, psychological and legal advice — particularly acting as if you have standing to speak officially for the church. Do you know what malpractice is? We could be sued for giving bad professional advice — and you could be criminally liable."

"I didn't —" sputtered the Sunday school superintendent. "Wait —"

"You had better stick to your very simple responsibilities," thundered the assistant pastor. "I have had great hopes for you. I've expected to put you on staff full-time. But it will make my superiors, the decision-makers of this church, doubt your judgment and spiritual maturity if it gets out that you jumped into something like this without asking for help — particularly if my son is hurt because of your blowing this thing, pretending as if you were a trained professional."

"But —" exclaimed the superintendent.

"If you even think about talking about this to anybody, keep in mind what Paul said about gossip-mongers. He lists them right up there with witches. I cannot express how angry I am. Let me caution you in Christian love, if I hear anything of this anywhere, I'm going to know where it came from. I'm not going to have you destroying a ministry, a life and a family with loose lips and poor judgment."

"But," sputtered the superintendent.

"My brother," thundered the assistant pastor. "I believe the Lord would have a word just for you. 'Yea, I would have you to submit yourself as never before to the discipline and authority of the Lord! Let not your soul be jeopardized by rebellion nor by loose talk. Be silent and know that I am God.'"

"Okay," sighed the superintendent. And he hung up.

Then, he began to get furious.

He could not sleep.

He moped around the house, unable to even tell his beloved wife what was troubling him so.

The more he thought about what had happened, the angrier he got.

He picked up the phone.

"Darrell," he said when the assistant pastor answered. "Listen carefully to me. Let's cut through the baloney right now. Your little boy, Matt, molested a little girl. He committed a sex crime.

"So, listen carefully. Until you get him some professional help, I don't want Matt to go anywhere near my Sunday school kids. He can stay downstairs in his Junior High class, but nowhere near the younger kids.

"Do you hear me? I don't want him helping in the classes. I don't want him assisting in the nursery. If he comes up the stairs to the younger kids' classes, I want you to come with him and stay with him until he returns downstairs."

The assistant pastor began to bluster.

"Darrell," interrupted the superintendent. "I want you to understand this as well: If I have any problems over this, I am going straight to the authorities. If I even hear a rumor that Matt is involved in anything else like this, I'll go to the police and tell them that you told me to keep my mouth shut — and that you would handle the situation.

"It's in your hands. You handle it. You make sure that your son gets help. And I'm going to be watching. You had better make certain that little Jeannie's family receives help, too, if you want me to stay out of this. Get them help. Because, if you can't, I will."

And he slammed down the phone.

He still felt terrible.

He had allowed himself to be trapped into the same conspiracy of silence that frequently keeps such scandals under the rug — and allows the perpetrators to go unpunished.

But what else could he do?

He didn't want to see a nice fourteen-year-old boy branded as a molester — particularly since it seemed entirely possible that the eight-year-old girl had propositioned him.

And the superintendent enjoyed his job at the church. He liked his place of authority. He didn't want to lose it.

For such reasons, it is so seldom that this sort of thing is reported.

Nobody wants to get involved.

Friends of the victim want to spare the child, the family, the church and the community the horrible humiliation of publicity.

Friends of the perpetrator out-do themselves as well, making sure that the secret doesn't get out and hurt innocent people.

This is so tragic, because in the vast majority of cases,

the offender will strike again — particularly if he gets no help. And there is a terrible thing called the "Vampire Syndrome." Not a medical condition, it is a sad phenomenon in which those who are molested often become molesters of children themselves.

Then, so many people are caught in the swirl of a society that makes millions of dollars exploiting sex. I'm not talking about porno. I mean blatantly erotic advertising for jeans, cars, soap and soda. I'm talking about an entertainment industry that has created sex myths like the "hooker-with-a-heart-of-gold" in movies ranging from the classic *My Little Chickadee* to Oscar winners such as *Klute, The Cheyenne Social Club* and *The Biggest Little Whorehouse in Texas,* and box-office smash hits such as *Trading Places, Total Recall,* or *Pretty Woman.* Listen, girls like that just aren't out there!

When I was on the street, hookers were invariably drugged-up, exploited, pitifully lonely, pathetic girls desperate for a different way of life. They were trapped, broke, emotionally tough as nails and quite often borderline crazy. They did not resemble what you see on TV — the business girl anxious to help folks out.

Sex sells, and so our entertainment industry has prostituted itself. In the 1950s, the public would pay millions to see such inspirational fare as *The Robe, The Ten Commandments* and *The Greatest Story Ever Told.* But quality was expensive. Sleaze is not.

Take ten teen-age girls in thong swimsuits, three sex-crazy boys cussing a lot, and a mad slasher with a butcher knife.

Mix them together with some blood, a little frontal nudity, glimpses of bare breasts and buttocks, and hints of kinky sex. The result? A low-budget cult movie guaranteed to gross $10 million at the box office.

On an airline flight to a recent crusade, I read a news article about an openly gay director's new movie — which I won't bother to publicize here — that featured the following:

• Young actor River Phoenix in a loincloth, posing on a crucifix as "G-String Jesus";

• Homosexual eroticism as Phoenix and actor Keanu Reeves portray pathetic boy street prostitutes "turning tricks to survive"; and

• Weird dialogue such as: "Why, you wouldn't even look at a clock unless hours were lines of cocaine ... or time itself was a fair hustler in black leather."

And let's not pretend that only bad people get hooked on this stuff! If I were a gossip, I could tell you names of politicians, evangelists, entertainers and public figures I have known who had to seek help for their private obsessions with porno magazines, dirty movies, bi-sexuality, prostitutes and other such sin.

One of the finest young evangelists I know recently had to take a year off to work in the secular world and patch up his marriage and his relationship with the Lord — after he got caught up in the secret excitement of looking at child pornography.

So, why are we surprised when our children are caught up in perverted play? Society bathes them in the giggles of illicit sex! Fashion tells them to be sexy — so the other third graders will like them! Even comic books now feature provocatively drawn, under-dressed super-heroes!

Why are we astonished when our children are easily seduced? Why do we wonder when they accept an opportunity to try it out for themselves? We've accepted filth as funny in our living rooms as we howl with laughter at the sex talk on *Cheers, Night Court, Married With Children, Three's Company, Anything But Love* and *Roseanne.*

Ours is a nation obsessed with sex, fixated on sex, and trapped into perverted distortions of this beautiful gift that God gave each man and woman.

Our kids are experimenting with what fan magazines, TV, movies, rock and country music, bestselling novels and advertising all tout to high heaven as wonderful! We're raising up a nation of confused little peeping Toms, exhibitionists, voyeurs, and porno addicts — thundering at them on the one hand that sex is bad, then giggling on the other hand that it is wonderful.

Then, when seduced, our kids naturally experience the heavy guilt, shame and confusion that is part of the package — not to mention herpes, VD, unwanted pregnancy and AIDS!

They are unable to cope. Like heroin addicts, they swear "to never do it again." They have a deep sorrow and remorse for what they have done.

But here the satanic seduction meets its goal: after you have sinned and sinned and sinned by doing something that gives such pleasure, you get caught up in a sorrow that is no longer unto repentance.

Instead, you begin to believe that there is no way out. You were born this way. God will never forgive you now.

And it doesn't matter.

Nothing does.

The joy of your sin is gone.

The excitement has faded.

Denial takes root.

The angry, bored search for something more exciting,

the bigger head-rush, a greater high, anything better, something more — begins.

Why do you think teen suicide is at the highest level in our nation's history? Our kids have given in to all the temptations we have spread before them and the shallow lies are too much.

Death looks better.

I am told that more than 3,000 high school girls get pregnant every day in the United States. Some are incest victims, taught sexuality by a sick family member. Others just fall for the lies that scream in their ears: Sex is the goal! Sex will make you mature! Sex will make you popular! Sex will give you something to brag about! Sex will land you a faithful knight in shining armor who will rescue you from the nightmare of your meaningless life!

How can you and I fight back as spiritual warriors?

We, as believers, must come to understand the tremendous confusion of the victims.

The emptiness.

The self-hate.

On one level, they know what they did was wrong — and they feel dirty and sinful.

On the other hand, what happened physically may actually have felt good. In many instances, the only warmth and love and affection that they have ever enjoyed was sexual.

Melissa — the woman who was taken into the home of the Christian physician and his wife — was considered to be a wonderful wife.

But she, too, had a terrible secret.

Throughout her childhood, she and her little sisters had been sexually abused by her grandfather.

Night after night as a child, Melissa submitted to her

grandfather's panting and pawing. Even worse, she had trembled in her bedroom, listening to the awful sounds of her little sisters also being abused. As they cried out, Melissa did not make a sound, but just closed her eyes, grateful it was not her turn.

At age fourteen, she escaped by intentionally getting pregnant by a neighborhood eighteen-year-old boy and manipulating him into a shotgun wedding. Soon after, her eleven-year-old sister committed suicide by jumping off of a railroad trestle. The other, thirteen years old, ran away and disappeared into the drug culture of the 1970s before surfacing years later as a pathetic, emotional cripple.

And Melissa lived with the pain of knowing she had just closed her eyes to her sisters' pain. She had turned her back on their torment. She had closed her mind and deadened her emotions.

But one night it all came back.

The nightmare returned with all the horror of a slasher movie. One night, Melissa heard familiar cries and whispers. In terror, she sat up and knew that her husband was molesting her seven-year-old daughter.

Biting her lip, she trembled in the dark — fearing for her younger daughter, age four.

But she did nothing.

The next morning, she went in and changed her seven-year-old's sheets. As gently as possible, she held her broken little girl and told her that it was her duty to obey and respect her daddy.

But things got worse.

Night after night, the horror continued. Melissa's husband would be a gentle, caring papa. Then, he would go cuddle with one of the girls and instead of it being a wonderful, bonding time between a child and daddy, the unthinkable would evolve in the darkness of the late evening.

Melissa sat in her bedroom, petrified, unable to intervene — and knowing that the other daughter was sitting up, too, her eyes filled with tears for her sister's pain.

One day, her husband bought a video camera. He told her how he had learned that incredible money could be made — by selling photographs of nude children and kids engaged in exotic sex acts.

Something snapped.

The next morning, Melissa loaded up her children, the new video camera and her husband's coin collection, then drove to the bank. There she took $4,500 in U.S. savings bonds out of the safe deposit box.

She emptied out the checking and savings accounts, then drove five hundred miles away to Dallas, Texas. In the phone book, she found the number of a shelter for abused women.

She called them, told her story — and was given instructions of where to come. There, she hid out for three weeks.

One Sunday night she was drawn to a nearby church — and answered the altar call.

She lived with the Christian physician and his wife for six weeks. They got her a job and an apartment. Today, she lives in suburban Fort Worth and continues to recover.

And her little girls are healing, too.

Incest is such a horrible thing.

It teaches a child there is such a thing as "evil love" — gentleness that really only hides selfishness and pain.

Understand now that we are not talking about the confusion of a promiscuous teen, but a molested child.

Often the child dearly loves the person who seduced them. Yet, at the same time they hate the person, too.

A rape victim needs counsel and Jesus, yes. But incest is so much worse. Amid the confusion and violence of a rape, the victim can feel angry at the attacker who hurt them.

But with incest, it is so much more difficult.

Consider the horror of being seduced by someone you love. Someone you look up to.

Someone you are supposed to obey.

Your dad.

Your big brother.

Your older cousin. Your uncle.

Your sister.

Consider the pain, the confusion, especially if the offender was gentle and patient and taught you to enjoy the experience.

Look at the destruction!

How can the little victim ever respect this person's authority or love again? How can the innocent one sort out what is good love and what is evil love.

Evil love? The term may seem impossible. Confusing. Wrong. Yet ... what else can a tender little heart call it?

When incest or molestation is exposed, the child may be called upon to testify against a loved one — a trusted part of his or her little life.

And then the child must live with the reality that because he or she gave in to the seduction, then tattled on the person they loved, that this person is in jail.

It's their fault.

It's so easy for you and me to hate a child molester —

to demand that this scum be locked away for life.

Yet the person who offended is also a child of God, struggling under the bondage of sin.

Jesus cared so for the victims of sex sin throughout His ministry on earth. How interesting that he publicly scorned the hypocritical religious leaders of his day, then unabashedly befriended the repentant street whores!

We must have the same mercy!

But our hearts cry out in anguish — for we must not be foolish, inviting wolves in to feed on our trusting flock!

Seek the Lord fervently before you venture into the dangerous waters of ministering to the horror of sexual sin.

Ask for the Lord's strength.

Yes, we can fight back. In power. In might. And in enormous effectiveness.

But pray for His wisdom.

Listen for His quiet, inner urging — for perhaps He will gently guide you to another calling. Perhaps your role will just be to merely love the victims and guide them to a qualified, Christian psychologist or psychiatrist.

This sort spiritual battle is so great. So easily you and I can get caught up in the emotions and the manipulations of the hurting ones. We can become co-dependents, actually getting in over our heads, enabling the offender to get away with sinning again.

And there are legal questions. If someone comes to you and confesses that they are committing crimes, you can be an accessory to the crimes if you do not report the matter at once to authorities. Yes, there are exceptions — particularly if you are a pastor or a professional counselor or an attorney and have the confidentiality shields that some states allow. But you had better know the law.

A small scandal can mushroom into a much larger one if it comes out that a church was protecting a child molester.

Your and my job must be to bring the love of Jesus Christ to the ones in anguish — to bring them the forgiveness and healing power of the Holy Spirit.

So, don't jump into a counseling situation.

There are professionals to whom some things must be given. Here, again, you can direct the person in need.

It is vital that psychological or psychiatric counseling be Christian. Secular psychology can do great harm. The healing power of Jesus is not offered. Occasionally, too, the doctor is sicker than the patient. In some schools of thought, incest and promiscuity are defended as natural expressions of love not understood by our up-tight society. You don't want someone you love further battered by such godless confusion.

For example, I know a preacher's wife who sought marriage counseling from a local psychologist. "Your self worth has been destroyed by your dogmatic husband's dominance," the non-Christian counselor told her. "You need to prove your independence to yourself. You need to find yourself a lover. Don't you know somebody that you really love? Somebody with whom you could have a really fulfilling, exciting, torrid affair?"

But there are good, Christian psychologists in most cities. You may be surprised to find that although they may be expensive, many will work with you for whatever your health insurance will pay. Others will accept whatever your budget allows.

As you gently love the victims, remember to be sensitive to their frailty. Often they have never had a good relationship that wasn't somehow tied to sexuality.

That may present a challenge in itself. You may find yourself being drawn into a sexual relationship as you attempt to help the hurting person. If so, seek counsel yourself — immediately! Get a qualified professional involved with the victim.

You're not going to help anyone by hurting them further!

What if you have been a victim?

What if you are reading this — wanting to know how to break out of the hurt, the cycle of sin and the lies of such a relationship?

Your story can have the same happy ending as Melissa's. The Christian physician's wife found Melissa a Christian psychologist who helped Melissa to understand that she had to admit a number of things to herself:

• I'm absolutely powerless when I come face-to-face with a molester. Although it has been the deepest desire of my heart, I could not do anything to stop my own molestation or that of my children.

• This nightmare has a terrible grip on my life and that of my children.

• I am in bondage to this sin and I want out.

• I cannot break out of this sin by myself.

• I can't blame my grandfather or my husband anymore — or my children or the economy or the sexually perverse media or the circumstances around me.

• I have to take measures to stop this sin — with God's help and seeking His protection from those who would hurt me and my children.

Why did Melissa have to go through such a litany?

So many adults in society today have difficulty owning up to responsibility. Melissa was responsible for a great deal. When she sat petrified in her bedroom and did nothing and when she told her seven-year-old to let Daddy have his way — she sinned.

She could have stopped the terror.

At the very least, she could have tried.

Melissa saw that she really did have trouble taking responsibility. For example, during the time her children were being molested, she would get in the car and drive 90 miles an hour in the middle of the night — often just for a mile or so on the interstate.

Why?

It gave her some sort of release.

One night, she was pulled over by a state trooper and issued a citation.

Melissa got angry at the policeman. It was his fault! He should have let her off! He knew she couldn't face her husband with a $125 speeding ticket!

She went to court and picked a fight with the judge — who threatened to cite her for contempt if she didn't quit weeping and blaming the trooper, the car manufacturer and her husband.

As she paid her fine, she got furious with the clerk, who was not exactly the brightest model of efficiency.

Nobody was good enough.

They were all idiots — inflicting pain on poor, helpless Melissa ... at least in her eyes.

She was trapped in an attitude of blaming everybody else in the world for her misfortunes: "It's not my fault, it's the cops' fault, it's the judge's fault, it's my husband's fault, my grandfather's fault."

Freedom begins when we say, "It's no one's fault but mine."

Melissa learned that as long as she believed she was entirely innocent and what happened was solely someone else's fault, she remained at risk.

As the victim of incest, she had to understand that her childhood incest was certainly not her fault. She was an innocent victim. But the sin continued after she became an adult — resulting in hurt to her own kids.

"It was not my fault that I was molested as a child. I was victimized," she says today. "Yet as an adult, I can make a choice — and I did, finally, make the right choice with God helping me."

Melissa found freedom when she stopped trying to justify herself. She fell entirely upon the mercy of the Lord.

She quit making excuses.

She acknowledged that God is right when he says that all have sinned and come short of His glory — there is none righteous, no not one.

The apostle Paul described himself as the chief of sinners. Once an evangelist was preaching on that passage and, afterwards, a woman came to him.

"Is that really true? Does the Bible really say that the chief of sinners got saved?"

The preacher said, "Yes, it does!"

And she said, "If the chief of sinners can get in, then I can, too!"

The blood of Jesus Christ works for every sinner, for every human being. The blood of Jesus can wash away any kind of sin.

There is no sin beyond His ability or His willingness to wash away.

Today, Melissa has done something else that is absolutely vital to recovery. She continues to fellowship with believers.

Her little girls adore the Christian physician and his wife — and call them Grandpa and Grandma.

Melissa has wisely re-entered the mainstream of society and doesn't identify herself as a former incest victim.

Such labels are unwise.

Sure, Melissa could have a ministry to incest victims by going public.

But her kids deserve to be able to leave the horror behind and not have to wallow in the tragedy of their past, reliving the horror of their abuse.

Her husband knows that at the women's shelter the children were examined and found to have all the signs of sexual abuse — one of the girls even had gonorrhea. The Christian physician, too, carefully documented his examinations of the children.

Because the gonorrhea had to be reported to health officials, the state welfare department eventually got involved and the girls had to make detailed statements of what had happened.

Fortunately, their mother had already moved them in with the well-respected, Christian physician's family — or else the girls might have been put into foster homes. As it was, no prosecution occurred since the crime occurred outside of the state of Texas.

But, their father knows, if Melissa were to return home and file charges, sufficient professional documentation exists to send him away to prison for decades.

He also knows that in many state prisons, child molesters have a six-month life expectancy. The other inmates despise the scum who would rape or seduce a child.

So, her husband is going along with her.

She has let him know that if he wants to try to get custody of the kids in court, he could lose everything — particularly his freedom. She lets them be with him as long as she is in the same room.

And he is never allowed to spend the night in the same building with them.

She has insisted he get counseling.

And he attends church now. Melissa says that her greatest hope for him is that if he keeps attending, he will be convicted of the Holy Spirit and will begin true healing, too.

The physician and his wife knew that Melissa simply had to have fellowship — particularly at the first, when she came back to the Lord. She needed the friendship and caring of other people.

It would not be the same to lock herself in her room and read self-help psychology books or watch religious TV.

She needed koinonia, the ancient Greek word for open, honest fellowship with believers of like precious faith. It's the kind of fellowship where Melissa can listen intensely as others share their heart and their feelings — the kind of fellowship where if she's out of line, her Christian brother or sister will love her enough to point it out to her.

It's the kind of fellowship where people pray for her, encourage her to be in church, and to be studying the word of God.

It's the kind of fellowship were people care about each other.

I've also seen this sort of fellowship out on the West Coast, in my Christian brother Sonny Arguinzoni's church and in the congregations he has helped start.

They, too, turn their homes into Holy Ghost hospitals, taking in new believers for six weeks and nurturing them in love and *koinonia*.

If you don't show up for church, people in Sonny's church will love you enough to call and find out what's wrong, were you sick, were you out of town, or are you just sitting at home feeling sorry for yourself.

I'm expecting great things from Melissa.

She's been through the fire.

Now, she's getting well. She's praying that the Lord will actually restore her marriage — and that He will heal the terrible rift between her girls and their Daddy. They need to love him.

And here's something incredible about Melissa: She's looking forward to the day when she can offer her home to somebody else who needs help.

She knows what it's like to be alone and helpless.

She's known the pain.

And the victory.

And this former emotional cripple who once did nothing as her own children were molested is ready to let her little apartment be a Holy Ghost hospital, too!

Yes, we can fight back with prayer and deliverance. We as Christians must learn how to overcome the powers of darkness. Incest is demonically inspired and the offender needs deliverance — and with God's help we can give it!

We have to face Satan and his demons in combat.

And we always win!

9

Your Home a Hospital

Are you willing to take a broken person to the Holy Ghost hospital?

Where is that hospital? It may be in your home.

How do we teach anyone to fight such injustice as the terrible assaults on small children described in the last chapter?

What kind of street fighters does Jesus want us to be? Matthew 5, 6 and 7 has one of the best checklists for the Christian warrior — no matter what spiritual battle you're facing. Put it to work and you'll be far more effective than you can ever be in your own strength and human wisdom.

Here's the list:

• *Blessed [and greatly to be envied] are the humble who rate themselves totally insignificant: for theirs is the kingdom of heaven.*

How can such a verse help you in a scandal such as the assistant pastor's son molesting the little girl?

Easy: If you don't get caught up in the seduction of personal status, you will be better able to do the right thing when you're in serious spiritual battle.

Let politics be so unimportant to you that you simply don't care if someone threatens to remove you from your valued position.

Accept the humble truth: If God wants you where you are, He will keep you there. So, do what is right — unworried that you might lose your reputation. Jesus cared so little for His reputation that he hung around with illiterate fishermen, socialized with dishonest tax-collectors, and allowed prostitutes to wash his feet with their tears. He washed away the sins of the world when he was executed amid the ridicule of foreigners, in public humiliation, nailed to two logs, hanging up in the air among thieves!

If your reputation or public status is not God-given, you don't want it anyway!

Don't think that you have all the answers, either. When someone you know or love is hurt in such a situation as this — either as a victim or offender — seek the Lord fervently. Where can you get help for this person? Support groups? Local counselors? A good book that explores the issue? Ask God to give you wisdom.

• *Blessed are they that mourn: for they shall be comforted.*

We must be able to cry. We must feel pain — and not harden ourselves. And we must seek healing from the One by whose stripes we are cured.

Hey, this isn't an easy one for me — macho Latino tough guy that I'd like to think I am.

But I know the truth: real men cry.

I must weep with those who weep. I must feel the pain

of the mother whose daughter is abused. I must ache with that confused little girl who thinks sex is a game! And I must hurt for that fourteen-year-old boy who molested her and must repent of this perversion and know — as only God can teach him — the purity and joy of sex in its proper place.

If I do that, I will find myself reacting like Jesus — rescuing the prostitute who was about to be stoned to death, calling out in friendship to Zacchaeus, the crooked tax collector, and reaching out in forgiveness to the thief beside Him on Calvary.

• *Blessed are the patient and slow to anger: for they shall inherit the earth.*

If you don't falsely accuse or publicly convict anybody, you'll be a mighty warrior. People will not be quick to accuse you unfairly, either. They will respect your judgment. They will not be afraid to follow you into battle — fighting beside you.

But what if we simply must respond to terrible sin? Well, follow the guidelines that Jesus gave us — and that we've already discussed in this book for confronting an offender. The same rules that work for satanists work for Christians.

• *Blessed are they who yearn for a closeness with the Father: for they shall be completely satisfied.*

There is such peace in the hearts of even the toughest warriors who seek God in the quietness of their own private time with Him.

My daily devotions are not just a time when I think blissful thoughts or try to concentrate on some obscure Scripture selected for me by a daily devotional guide. No! It is a time when I take all my troubles and problems and worries to the Creator of the Universe!

Guess what? He has answers.

He will calm your troubled heart.

He wants you to know Him, too! No matter what crisis you are facing, when you can take it to Him in absolute privacy — just you and Him, one-on-one, it fades.

He will restore your mind, giving you mental quickness and clarity of mind.

And He will knock down your Walls of Jericho and part your Red Sea. After all, who can come against you when you've got Him on your side?

You're tattling to the One who sets everything right! He may chide you for being wrong. And He will comfort you when you admit your stupidity.

But He will ride to your rescue much faster than the U.S. Cavalry.

And He will cover you with loving protection.

• *Blessed are the merciful: for they shall receive mercy.*

Don't be quick to convict.

Someday, you will benefit from somebody who will just decide not to prosecute.

Is that fair?

Is that just? Well, aren't you glad you haven't been prosecuted for everything that you ever did? I did things that today I still must not talk about.

I have confessed them to my Lord.

And I live in joy that He did not choose to see me in prison. Instead, he forgave me.

And so, I must forgive others — particularly when they do lousy stuff to me. I pray for them.

And I put the matter in God's hands.

Seek the Lord before trying to take revenge or see somebody punished. Prayerfully, go before Him. Let your anger rest.

• *Blessed are the pure in heart: for they shall see God.*
Amen!

And keep reading, my friends:

• *Blessed are the peacemakers and maintainers of peace for they shall be called the sons of God.*

• *Blessed are they which are persecuted for doing good: for theirs is the kingdom of heaven.*

• *Blessed are you when men shall ridicule you, and persecute you and shall say all kinds of false and evil things about you because you believe in Me. Rejoice and be joyful! Great is your reward in heaven, for in the same way they persecuted the prophets of historical times.*

The checklist found in Matthew 5, 6 and 7 continues. Read it for yourself in your own Bible. Here are some of my personal favorites.

• Don't bind yourself by vows or oaths. Let your Yes be Yes and your No be simply No.

• Do not resist the evil man who injures you; but if anyone strikes you on the cheek, turn to him the other one, too.

• If anyone wants to sue you and take your shirt, let him have your coat, too. And if someone forces you to carry their load a mile, go with him two miles.

• Love your enemies and pray for those who persecute you to show that you are the children of your Father who is in heaven. After all, if you love only those who love you, what reward can you have? And if you greet only your friends, what more than the heathen are you doing?

• Do your good deeds quietly and without any publicity.

• Don't be anxious, saying "What are we going to have to eat?" or "What are we going to have to wear?" Your heavenly Father knows well that you need them all. But instead, seek first His kingdom and His righteousness and all these things will be taken care of.

• Don't judge or condemn others and they won't criticize you, either.

• Watch out for false prophets. You will recognize them by their fruits. A good tree cannot bear worthless fruit. Neither can a diseased tree bear excellent fruit. And so it is with teachers of truth: examine the fruit of their labors.

Wow!

These are the keys to effective Christian battle.

How can this be? This looks like a prescription for becoming a wimp!

No, the Lord knew what He was talking about.

He knew that God built you and me in a special way. He knew we are happier when we obey these rules — when we make peace, don't worry, and are pure of heart! All sorts of blessings and power are ours when we are patient, slow to anger, merciful, yearning for closeness with God, nonjudgmental and humble!

Who can do all this, however?

You can.

Jesus did.

And how did Jesus fight back?

By putting all these rules, starting with the simple "blesseds" into every day practice!

As a result, was He just a mamby-pamby wimpo who let tough guys push him around?

Not hardly!

Look at Matthew 12 and 16 when false teachers tried to provoke Him into doing something for which they could arrest Him.

Loudly they accused him of being Satan for performing

miracles — in this case, casting out demons. Well, Jesus fired back, "You vipers! A kingdom at war with itself always loses. A house divided against itself cannot stand. So, if Satan were to cast out devils, he would be divided against himself. No, I cast out devils by the Spirit of God. How can you, being so evil, pretend to speak good things here? You're just a bunch of snakes!"

Not exactly the response of a lily-livered pansy.

Hard words.

They cut the offenders deeply — but gave them a chance to change their nasty ways. The Bible mentions a number of leaders who ended up following Jesus, such as Nicodemus and Joseph of Arimathea.

So, what does this have for you and me?

We must stand up to evil!

Jesus didn't challenge anybody to step outside to go a couple of rounds. Instead, He took on His enemies in righteous anger — and with wise mercy!

In the Garden of Gethsemane, he scolded Simon Peter, who pulled a sword and began to defend his Lord and Master with cold steel. Instead, Jesus humbly submitted to the abuses and scorn of His enemies.

And in the process, in His obedience to the Father's orders, He fulfilled thousands of years of prophecy, won eternal salvation for you and me, and defeated Satan for all time!

By living the "blesseds."

This stuff works!

Consider how it worked with Lesleye. After years of terrible abuse by a strangely unpredictable and frequently irrational husband, Lesleye took her small daughter and fled her home one day.

To buy groceries, Lesleye sold her own blood at a

plasma center on skid row. It was there that she saw a flyer about a city center for the homeless. Ashamed, she took her little daughter, Tonya, and checked in.

They were given an army cot in an old, unheated warehouse, partitioned off from 35 other destitute women and their kids by makeshift room dividers built by volunteers.

In the shelter, Lesleye prayed, "Lord, I need help. I don't even know for what to ask. But I need help. Protect me, Father! Send me somebody who will show me what you want me to do."

Why such a prayer?

Because that was what she required. She needed a friend — a godly friend who would show her how to make life work.

But such new friends are not found on every street corner. In fact, anyone pretending to be such is worthy of your extreme caution. Yet in her extreme vulnerability, that was what Lesleye sought.

A middle-aged social worker named Agnes one Monday sat across from Lesleye and little Tonya in the day-care center of the shelter and knew that this family was different.

They were not merely homeless. They were not the chronic poor that Jesus told us to love, to care for ... and to know that they would always be among us.

No, these two were different.

Although Agnes was no spiritual giant, no Joan of Arc hearing voices from heaven, no Corrie ten Boom filled with mighty resolve to resist the Nazis, Agnes heard from the Lord.

It was not an easy word that she heard deep within her spirit. "Take these people home with you and love them like your own children," was the message.

Agnes winced in disbelief as she bounced little Tonya on her knee. No, she couldn't take this child and her mother home.

That ran against everything she'd ever learned in her 40 years of social work. Take a client into her home? No.

No, she knew not to get emotionally involved. She had to be professional, detached, clinical and impartial.

She knew she had to be able to leave matters of the job at the job every evening — and to enjoy her private life, separate from her professional life.

She deserved it.

She couldn't start dragging home stray puppies.

But then, unexpectedly, she sat next to Lesleye and Tonya in church the following Sunday. She was friendly and detached.

But as the congregation sang, Agnes saw the tremendous pain and heartache on Lesleye's face.

And she knew that she had heard the Lord correctly. She was supposed to love Lesleye and Tonya.

Like her own children.

Agnes invited the two to lunch.

And in a little fast-food restaurant, as Agnes listened to Lesleye's story, her heart was touched. She invited them home.

They became the closest of friends in a very short time. Agnes suggested that Lesleye bury herself in the Scripture, filling her heart and mind and soul with the reality of God's marvelous promises.

It has not always been easy. At one point, when Lesleye sank into a deep depression and did not want to leave her bedroom, Agnes had to get tough. She ordered Lesleye out of the house and told her that she could not return until she had applied for a job at five different firms that day.

When Lesleye refused, ashamed of how badly she looked without her front teeth — which had been knocked out the day that she fled — Agnes knelt with her in prayer.

"I don't have the money it will take to buy you a dental bridge," she told her. "And neither do you. However, God does."

Indeed, that day as Lesleye swallowed her pride and looked for work, Agnes looked for a government agency that would provide dental work.

She found two different programs.

And before Lesleye started a part-time job at Burger King that weekend, she had a temporary appliance that kept her from looking like a hillbilly.

Was Lesleye angry at being forced to get a job?

Yes, at first.

But then, as her self-worth returned from meeting the public, doing a good job and getting recognition from her boss, Lesleye could not believe that someone like Agnes existed.

Agnes had showed her — not with words, but with actions — that it is possible for a single woman to survive without being terribly lonely. She showed through her life how, indeed, Jesus could be the high priest of a family.

And Agnes unknowingly turned her home into a Holy Ghost Hospital as she showed Lesleye how to fight back by arming herself with the Holy Scripture and the power of God within her.

Enveloped with His love and with Agnes' patient care, Lesleye soon left intensive care.

Consider how this concept worked with Astrid.

Astrid is a beautiful woman, the type that turns heads in a crowd. She is tall and composed — with ebony hair and dark Hispanic eyes, flashing, friendly and full of concern.

You would expect to find her on a runway in an international beauty pageant representing Chile or Italy or maybe Mexico with her flowing hair, her ruby-red lips, and perfect make-up that appears as if she wears none at all.

She moves with elegance, demonstrating tremendous self-confidence — yet with a hint of unspoken tragedy. In those beautiful, empathetic eyes is caution from a deep, long-ago hurt.

She is so beautiful that women are often wary of her. Men are frequently intimidated by her. She is too perfect. She looks like a New York model who accidentally got out of her limousine at the wrong address.

But her real beauty flows from somewhere down within her, beautifully from a spirit consciously yielded to the mighty Lord to whom she has given everything. She is truly a servant of God, quietly willing to help someone who is hurting — even if it means opening her home to them.

What people don't know is that Astrid has been through the fire, too.

She was raised in Chile, a beautiful South American coastal country more than twice the length of California with a population of 12.5 million or so.

It is a diverse country with some of the world's highest mountains and greatest ocean depths, but a generally mild, Mediterranean-like climate.

Astrid was raised in a fine middle-class home. But,

when she was nineteen, she fell in love. The pulse of passion was raised, and in a storm of desire she left her will unprotected, ignored the consequences and found herself with child. Against the wishes of her family, Astrid decided to keep the baby.

By the time Astrid was twenty-one, she was working for a major airline. She began flying back and forth between the U.S. and South America — and she dreamed of raising her little daughter, two-year-old Celeste, in the United States, the land of opportunity. Celeste was the inspiration and joy of her life. Astrid wanted more for her than Chile could provide.

So, Astrid sought permission to come to America with her little daughter — as permanent residents. In the U.S., she stayed with relatives, perfected her English and got a good job. She had a tremendous mind for business and a determined will. With no financial backing at all, she started her own catering firm.

After eighteen long, hard-fought months, she was financially independent with an excellent following of faithful customers who simply would not have anyone else cater their banquets, birthdays, weddings, anniversaries, and Bar Mitzvahs. From nothing, she had built a profitable company with her skill, reputation and market sense. People were drawn to her because of her honesty, dependability, and elegance.

Then, she met the man that she hoped would fulfill her dreams. She wanted what many women desire, to settle down permanently and love a husband who would care and provide for her.

She wanted someone she could trust and respect. One dream was to combine her talents with his, to build up a prosperous business with him.

But she did at least one thing wrong: She didn't seek God about the man. She didn't ask the Lord whether she should marry this knight in shining armor.

What followed was a horrible nightmare!

In actuality he was a smooth-talking, manipulating, slick Casanova. He had pursued her with promises and conned her with gifts and flowers.

One bad deal after another on his part revealed his true nature ... he was a crook! Nevertheless, Astrid stayed with him.

It wasn't long before he mercilessly began to beat and abuse Astrid. He became as a vicious animal, full of hatred. He degraded her to the pits of nothingness. There were many times she was locked in her room for days on end.

Sometimes the after-effects of the beatings would drain her for weeks. All during this time, she would call upon God, begging Him for strength to endure this affliction.

She remembered her childhood days of being raised in a Christian home. But, her own will to stand up and fight against this monster eventually disappeared. Gradually, losing heart, she settled into a state of resignation, accepting her sentence. She desperately wanted to escape his never-ending torture, but was petrified of the consequences.

Astrid soon became lost in this devastating world of torment which left her hopeless and disillusioned. He would grab her by the wrists, throw her against the wall and beat her face with her fists until her delicate skin was torn and bleeding.

Astrid would twist in agony as she lay gasping for breath. Sometimes, he would throw her onto the bed and tie her limbs to the bedposts, leaving her bruised and bound, and sometimes unconscious.

Astrid would look into his eyes, desperately searching for any shred of humanity or compassion. What she found staring back at her was the icy glare of a devil only too willing to cast her into the dungeons of hopelessness.

The apostle Paul describes such people as those whose consciences are seared with a hot iron.

And little Celeste, watching fearfully, did not escape the horror.

What had happened?

Astrid had believed the lies of American movies and television. She had come to the United States in search of utopia.

Prosperity.

The American dream, as perverted by those who buy and sell.

Here she could earn enough money to buy any happiness. But, instead, it bought her unspeakable terror.

Where had she gone wrong?

She had put money and success on an altar and worshiped them, dreaming of the day when she would take her place among the beautiful women of the "Dallas," "Dynasty" and "Days of Our Lives" reruns.

But it was all an empty lie.

She had left God back in Chile — and why not? Nobody in the glittery, tinsel-town fairy tales of the silver screen ever praised or worshiped the Lord. There, clergymen were crazies, criminals, con-men or clowns. Believers were backward, superstitious old women and unsophisticated fools.

Real people worshiped success.

They gloried in torrid romance.

They reveled in prosperity.

And they lived with abandon — in financial bliss, material abundance and emotional exhilaration.

But Astrid's world wasn't like that.

She was in a very real human hell.

She cried out for death.

But it did not come.

She fought back in anger and pride. And was slapped down every time. Resentfully, she plotted her husband's murder. Maybe, like on TV, she would douse him with gasoline while he slept — then stand back and watch him burn.

No jury on earth would convict her, she wept. But — she was no murderer. Defeated, she began planning her own suicide. But what about Celeste? She couldn't leave this precious child in this nightmare.

One day, Astrid fled with Celeste.

For weeks they hid in a cheap motel. Her wicked husband sold her business, left town with all the money, and stuck the missing Astrid with all the bills.

Alone in their little hotel, Celeste would sit in her mother's lap, her eyes wide with wonder as Astrid recounted the cherished Bible stories of her own childhood. Celeste's favorites became the ones about the baby Moses, and especially baby Jesus.

Celeste's eyes lit up like Christmas lights when she heard how God's protection was upon the lives of these babies. As she drifted off to sleep, little Celeste would reflect on the beautiful tales and on the greatness and faithfulness of God. She would dream that she was one of the precious children that Jesus gathered in His lap, and there she would be safe from any harm.

And her mother cried as she softly sang the child's

favorite songs, "Jesus Loves the Little Children," and "Jesus Loves Me, This I Know For the Bible Tells Me So."

But they had no money. No catering business. No credit. No reputation.

No home.

No hope.

Astrid did the only thing she could.

She fought back ... on her knees!

Where else could she go but to the One who never forgets His children? Astrid sought the Lord as she had never before.

And He met her where she was.

He loved her.

He gave her protection — despite her stubbornness and pride.

He soothed her tortured mind — despite her deep anger and seething resentment.

And He gave her protection. She really had no choice but to depend on His mighty provision to deliver her from an earthly hell far worse than anything movie-makers ever conjured up.

She lacked any confidence that God would speak to her. So, she sought a friend who could hear His voice.

The Lord did send such a person — Edna with whose help Astrid bounced back with a newfound self-confidence and rekindled trust in the Lord.

She was free to soar like a bird through the boundless expanses of the heavens. Carrying a Bible in her purse everywhere she went, Astrid filled her mind with the promises of the Lord. Jesus Christ walked into the fortress of her soul and became her prince—the Prince of Peace.

Today, Astrid is an out-patient at Edna's Holy Ghost

hospital. She has her own apartment. On cold nights, bad memories come back, but she has learned to call upon God. She keeps her mind on the Word, depending daily on the Lord. And through her own pain, she is able to empathize with other people's pain and can offer comfort.

It's in helping others that she forgets her pain.

She has even learned to trust again. She has friends who are men, although she is understandably hesitant about remarrying. Some things come with time.

There have been tough times.

Despite the good Christian influences all around her, Celeste became a frightened, fragile, nervous adolescent, which eventually let to the devastating eating disorder *bulimia*.

Bulimia — like anorexia — deceives the sufferer into believing she is fat and must lose weight in order to be beautiful. Bulimia brings with it an abnormal constant craving for food, and a desperate need to vomit up the food or pass it quickly through misuse of laxatives, so as to avoid weight gain.

It leads girls into a cycle of pigging out and "purging" — getting rid of the food unnaturally, which can severely disrupt the digestive system and damage a young body.

Astrid has tried to soften her pain, watching her daughter, searching for answers — *Why me? Why us? Why now?*

It didn't seem to matter how beautiful little Celeste was, she saw herself as fat and ugly. Her mother stayed there, frustrated, sobbing with her, wishing that she was God, that she could stop her daughter's anguish and kiss her wounds away.

Astrid did the only thing she could.

She fought back.

On her knees through prayer!

Today, Celeste is a model, and has inherited her mother's business finesse. Graduating with a master's degree in business administration at twenty-four years of age, she stepped into a very lucrative job and is climbing the corporate ladder.

In spite of this success, she still has reoccurring nightmares, but her mother is still there to comfort and pray with her.

Yet I know that she will emerge victorious, for they both rejoice in the mercies of their heavenly Father.

Do you have the courage to be an Edna for the Astrids out there? For the Melissas? For the Marcs?

Have you made God that offer?

Astrid still has a tough battle and a long road ahead of her. The scars of the past haunt her at times.

Today, both Celeste and Astrid know Jesus in a special way. They have seen his goodness through the kindness of His obedient servant — a simple believer ... who was willing to care.

Will you be an Edna?

What may be expected of you?

• You must be willing to give, never expecting to be repaid. Remember that when Jesus healed the ten lepers, only one came back and thanked Him.

• You must love, not expecting any love in return. Real love, Jesus' love has no strings attached.

• You must respect and care about unrespectable and hard-to-care-about people who have been rejected by society — and themselves.

• Unselfishly, you must keep their well being in mind — and care more about their success than your own.

• You must be faithful with an unconditional love. That means, you must love the person when they are angry and defiant — as well as when they are grateful and loving in return.

• You must be worthy of confidence, trustworthy, and able to keep terrible confessions of sin and heartache to yourself. Their past must be safe with you. You cannot gossip. Not even to your closest friend.

Can you be an Edna?

Can you turn your home into a Holy Ghost Hospital?

You may get hurt. The ones you bring into your Emergency Room may steal from you. They may sell marijuana from your back door. They may move in and refuse to leave. Their children or pets may destroy your most beloved possessions. They may run up your long-distance telephone bill and wreck your car.

You may have to learn tough love — demanding accountability from them.

They may denounce you in public as a vicious, heartless wretch — or a foolish goody-goody with a messiah compulsion to save the world.

You may have to attend Alcoholics Anonymous or other self-help support groups with them — since they may not have the willpower to go alone.

And you may never get any thanks or recognition. Your reward may only be in heaven.

You see, there are very few Astrids out there. There are a lot of failures who will always be failures.

Astrid is a rare success story.

And maybe that's all that God will give you — glorious, heart-warming successes. Or maybe you will be called to serve the failures who will ache to be back on the streets, unable to accept your love, to believe that Jesus wants to hold them to His arms, unable to see that life can be good and joyful and fulfilling.

You'll have to show them.

As you do, you may snatch one more precious child of God from the jaws of hell and the earthly torments of Satan.

More than that, you may be doing incredible battle that you cannot see with your human eyes. Do you suppose the Sunday school teacher who led Billy Graham to Jesus knew right then and there that she was changing the world?

Do you suppose the pastor who took time with little Johann Sebastian Bach suspected that he was filling the churches of the next three centuries with the music of joy and godly desire?

As you change just one life, you may be changing all of history.

You may not hear the screams of hellish fury.

But you will be fighting back more effectively than any who turn their backs on the unloved, the unwashed, the unwanted.

You will be fighting back.

In power

And obedience.

10

Gaining Greater Power

Ho Chi Minh, like China's Mao Tse-tung, was an avid reader of an ancient textbook called *The Art of War* by a Chinese general named Sun Tzu who won brilliant military victories across China in the year 500 B.C.

Among Tzu's basic philosophies is that a limited war is absurd, that "war is an act of violence pushed to its utmost bounds" and that the effective warrior absolutely, positively must know as much as possible about the enemy. From studying your opponent's culture, religion, folklore, traditions and history, you need to know — for example — how he reacts to impossible odds:

• Does he turn and run to fight another day?

• Does he surrender? If so, does he subvert the efforts of his captors to rule over him — and thus, should he, when captured, be killed?

• Does he when outnumbered "go out in a blaze of glory," trying to take as many opponents with him as possible?

• Or does he summon the courage of a cornered rat and scrap his way out — seizing victory from a stunned and over-confident enemy?

The apostle Paul advises us that as effective spiritual warriors, we must size up the opposition. (2 Cor. 2:11)

So, how can we understand Satan's tactics?

Don't waste your time with the contradictory exaggerations and empty claims written by various Satanists. That's not how you will learn how Satan wages war.

Instead check out what God tells us about the devil's tactics:

• Ephesians 6:12 warns us that "we are not battling physical opponents, but against evil, supernatural powers, the rulers of this world's present darkness, spirit forces of wickedness in the air." So, in battling Satan, much more will be accomplished interceding on your knees than with a M-1 rifle in your hands.

• Matthew 4 shows how Satan attempted to woo Jesus with flattery and suggestions that Jesus commit seemingly "victimless" sins. Satan hasn't changed, my friends! This is exactly the sort of stuff with which he hits you and me today!

• Look at John 8:44 where Jesus warned his disciples that Satan "is a liar. There is no truth in him." Absolutely! And one of his favorite tactics is to wrap a little truth in a lot of lies so that you and I are seduced by the ounce of truth!

• He is subtle and full of evil mischief. He is an enemy of anything that turns out good. He loves to pervert the way that the Lord set up things to work. (Acts 13:10)

• He will lose his last battle against God and will be punished — tormented for all eternity — and will not be able to trouble us any longer (Rev. 20:10).

And he is a good fighter.

So, let's ponder a few of the world's tactics of warfare by looking at Tzu's tactics used by the North Vietnamese to frustrate the United States.

These cannot be our tactics. But it is wise for us to know how the world fights back. All successful warfare is based on deception, according to Tzu. That's exactly how the Prince of Lies works, too, my friend.

Satan and his forces will:

- avoid you when you are strong and able;
- try to confuse and anger your leaders, and to disrupt your alliances — and if you are united, work to divide your forces against each other, for the highest accomplishment is to get you to fight among yourselves and defeat yourself;
- encourage you to be falsely self-assured, overconfident and arrogant;
- when you are under strain, wear you down to complete exhaustion, confusion and defeat;
- do whatever possible to keep you from seeing any victory that would boost your morale.

Such deception! Such evil intrigue!

So many people are held in bondage by fear. You're about to be fired because of your Christian witness, it tells you. You're going to get sick because the devil picks on Christians. You're not going to be able to pay your bills. You're going to fail publicly and be held up for ridicule.

Fear.

Paralyzing fear. But in reality, the Christian has no need to fear anything — as you saw with the Christians in Island Pond and Mannatu Crossing.

See, overcoming fear and replacing it with a solid

trust in the Lord's goodness, His mercy, His protection and the glory of His plan for you is not some idle boast.

It's not a positive-thinking platitude, an inspirational thought.

It's straight from God's Word:

• "God is faithful and will strengthen you and protect you from Satan." (2 Thess, 3:3)

• "I can do all things through Him who strengthens me." (Phil. 4:13)

So, can we pay God to protect us and fight our battles for us?

What a silly question, you may ask. But that's how Satan worshipers think. If they do sufficient evil, they believe, they will earn the right to rule in hell with Satan and his demons.

Unfortunately for them, of course, they're going to roast for all eternity like anybody else who rejects Jesus.

But they think they'll be treated special once they get to hell. My dad thought so.

If you read my book, *Devil on the Run,* you will know he was a dramatic spiritualist healer back in the tropical forest of our Caribbean island. Over seven decades, he paid dearly, trying to do the bidding of the evil forces that yanked him around — and rewarded him by mystically doing his bidding.

He could summon horrible demonic forces.

But he was not a master of the supernatural.

The evil forces were his master.

They tormented, disappointed and taunted him throughout his life — then threatened to kill him if he turned to Jesus.

He had to do their bidding.

And that's how some people look at Christianity. They

think that if they live some poverty-and-penitence lifestyle, never break any of the Ten Commandments, carry around a three-pound King James Bible, and wear a holy scowl on their faces or say "Well, praise the Lord!" with every other breath, the Lord will answer their prayers more promptly.

Just think about people you know who have tried to bargain with the Lord. Foxhole conversions. People who came to Jesus as their airliner plummeted toward disaster. If He will only do this or that, they'll donate half of their savings or give the rest of their lives to church work or such.

Another sad lie being taught these days is that if you pay God a certain amount, He will bless you more than before. What a perversion of the tithes and offerings promises! I guess what really irks me is that you and I are supposed to send our "seed faith" gift to the televangelists preaching this perverted principle nonstop every time you turn on the tube.

Why don't they tell us to plant a seed with our local congregation, the struggling ministry of our choice or some orphanage in India? Because *they* want our cash!

What does God say about all this?

Once upon a time there was a man named Simon, who according to Acts 7 "had formerly practiced magic arts" in Samaria.

People there all regarded him with great respect, from the lowest peasant to the highest official — believing that he had incredible, dazzling power.

But when they heard the good news about Jesus, many became Christians — even Simon. And after being baptized, he devoted himself constantly to the deacon evangelist Philip.

"After seeing miracles of great power performed by Philip, he was utterly amazed," the text says. "Now when the apostles in Jerusalem heard that many in Samaria had accepted the gospel, they sent Peter and John to them.

"And the two prayed for many Samaritans that they might receive the Holy Spirit."

When Simon saw that the Holy Spirit was imparted through the laying on of the apostles' hands, he brought money and offered it to them, asking:

"Please grant me also this authority in order that anyone on whom I place my hands may receive the Holy Spirit."

And was the Lord pleased?

Not at all!

Peter said to him, "May you and your money rot! You cannot buy God's free gift! Repent of this depravity and pray that your conniving heart may be forgiven."

To be an effective fighter, don't get bogged down in money or possessions, the Bible also warns. "Do not gather for yourself possessions here on earth where moth, rust and worm destroy and where thieves break in and steal," warns Matthew.

"Remember: nobody can serve two masters. He will hate one and love the other or he will be devoted to one and neglect the other."

You cannot serve both God and riches.

What does the Lord really want from you?

You. Living in His simple lifestyle. Generous to those in need. Humble. Gentle. Patient. Slow to anger.

What's that?

Are we really supposed to turn the other cheek when somebody punches us?

I'm sure you've heard Christians joke: "Sure, I'll turn the other cheek. But if that guy hits me again, look out!"

As a young Christian, I learned from real-life experience that I was not supposed to go get a gun or knife and defend myself — even if I was in mortal danger.

Over and over, I saw the Lord taking care of me when old street enemies came to kill me and were powerless against the protection of the Almighty.

One time in particular, a longtime enemy whose face I had scarred for life attacked me. When I reached to grab a car antenna — which makes a good weapon when you've got nothing else — my Christian girlfriend screamed to me that I wasn't supposed to fight back.

And the Lord protected me.

But what does the Bible really say about you or me fighting back?

"Behold, I give unto you power to tread on serpents and scorpions, and over all the power of the enemy: and nothing shall by any means hurt you," declares Luke 10:19.

We have been given immense power.

God will move mountains.

But you have to remember He's the one doing it.

Sure, you say, the Bible says all that, but —

What about ...

Sickness?

Or **disgrace?**

Or *poverty!?*

If you try, you can find something really scary — something that you can really fear.

Maybe it's cancer.

Or bankruptcy.

Or maybe after reading this far, you're completely intimidated by the evil wiles of that powerful, fallen angel, the prince of the earth, Satan.

You can spend much of your life trembling in fear over Satan's terrible, humanistic, demonic world out there.

Some Christians believe that if we just leave him alone, he will leave us alone. They wallow in their terror. You can almost hear the delighted, hilarious laughter from hell's gates.

Don't trust, whisper the evil voices: fear us.

Praise God! We have been given the same power as Jesus had to fight the demons of hell. When we accepted Jesus Christ as our Savior and were filled with the Holy Spirit, our inward power was complete.

He told us that we could control the demons of hell and with our hands heal the sick.

We are told in Matthew 16:18 that whatever we bind on earth will be bound in heaven and whatever we loose on earth will be loosed in heaven.

This spiritual authority was given to us as believers today. Therefore, let us declare war on the devil. Let's be on the offensive, bringing deliverance and the power of the living Christ to those in need.

We must not be afraid but we must seek a battlefield and armed with the Word and the Holy Spirit pursue Satan and his demons and push them back to the gates of hell.

Believe that our soon returning Lord through us will strike terror in the hearts of His enemies.

Don't wait for the devil to hit you — Hit him first!

11

The New Age Movement

Fear is exciting to some Christians.

Why else do people go to horror movies? Because fear is fun. It is seducing.

Few Christians realize how wallowing in real fear can cause us to take our eyes off of the Lord.

For example:

Is a terrible conspiracy making broad the way for the Antichrist? Are rainbows the secret symbols of God-haters whose teachings have ensnared Christianity's top leaders? Perhaps you've heard of the New Age movement.

A growing number of Christians are scared to death of it. Why else do they gather in seminars, growing ever more fearful of the power of the Antichrist as they take down lists of alleged participants in the New Age plot — ranging from comic book publishers to TV producers, from motivational authors to Christian food-for-the-hungry organizations?

Why all the fear?

Most Christians caught up in it would not tell you that it is fun.

They're terrified.

They're convinced of the power of the devil and blinded to the majesty and dominance and absolute Lordship of our great Creator.

What, exactly, is the New Age movement?

"Every few decades, a new American religion emerges to suit the spiritual needs of restless people," wrote reporter Marilyn Geewax in a recent edition of the *Atlanta Constitution* newspaper. "Just since the early 1970s, another new faith has sprouted: The New Age movement. A 'new age for humanity' began to appear in 1971 with the publication of a book, *Be Here Now,* by Baba Ram Dass.

"Two decades later, the movement has become a major force, with millions of faithful. But many people have trouble understanding New Age. That's because it isn't a formal religion, but rather an amalgam of theories and therapies.

"Generally, the movement's goal is the widespread development of a mystical consciousness that connects nature and humanity," wrote the journalist. "Individuals transform themselves through various spiritual techniques, often involving meditation, yoga, vegetarianism and rituals.

"Individuals are supposed to strive for 'wellness' by healing themselves, which in turn helps heal the planet. Harmonic convergences pass wellness between the Earth and adherents.

"If you're thinking: 'Huh?' that's understandable.

"But New Age may turn out to be a dangerous idea for

our times," continues Geewax. "While encouraging an obsessive interest in one's self, the movement shows scant interest in doing something for others.

"New Agers may plaster their bumpers with stickers admonishing others to 'visualize peace,' but do they ask themselves to do the work of peace? While Catholic nuns operate orphanages in El Salvador, New Agers attend workshops called 'Crystals, Magnets and Vibrational Healing.'

"...The movement itself puts no emphasis on personal sacrifice," writes the *Atlanta Constitution* reporter. "People are encouraged to believe they are doing something for the environment and world peace when in fact they are just pondering, not acting. Give me the Shakers. At least they built great chairs."

Is the New Age movement something that deserves serious consideration by thinking Christians? Dare we just look away?

Most believers had never heard of it until a number of Christian books came out in 1983 detailing various aspects of the alleged threat. Then a number of speakers and authors began lecturing on the subject — as shocked church members jotted notes and vowed that they would not donate to certain charities, would not buy certain books, would not purchase certain children's toys or corporations' products and so forth.

Speakers alleged that the New Age movement has permeated the thought of many Christian leaders — that unknowingly have begun to promote the New Age's satanic philosophies.

Some speakers still name specific names — charging some highly respected Christians and organizations with falling under the subversive influences of what they say is a terrible conspiracy to usher in the Antichrist.

One group mentioned from time to time is a noted campus fellowship and its publishing house. Admitting that the group has enjoyed an impeccable reputation in the past, one author admitted publicly, "much that appears to be New Age-oriented has come out of that organization in recent years."

Many speakers attack such concepts as inner healing, objecting to the use of the term "holistic," which refers to the whole person — body, mind and soul. Such principles are hardly new. "Teaching the whole man," is a motto of one major Christian university, for example.

However, some Christians caught up in the initial announcements, denunciations, accusations and finger-pointing seem to be backing away.

One popular women's speaker says she no longer lectures about the New Age movement. She's still convinced that there is an occult conspiracy called the New Age movement. She has an extensive collection of such occult books as Marilyn Ferguson's *The Aquarian Conspiracy*. In that book, Mrs. Ferguson proposes wide-ranging plans for the remaking of society — a world of "unity" in which all religions and philosophies would be examined for their worthwhile points. A new humanistic society would rise, putting to work the best of Hinduism, Buddhism, Taoism, spiritualism, animism — but not necessarily the "non-coexistant" monotheistic religions, such as Islam, Judaism or Christianity.

She also has copies of books by Helena Petrovna Blavatsky, who started the Theosophical Society in 1875 and told of a "New Age" when humans would seek out and be guided by spirits who would manifest themselves as "masters" — which she said would be either spirit beings or fortunate men who had become more highly evolved.

But this noted Christian lecturer says that Christians have been warned about this sort of thing for 2,000 years.

It's hardly new.

The apostle Paul warned the church at Colossi, "Beware of anyone getting hold of you by means of theosophy which is specious make-believe on lines of human tradition, corresponding to the elemental spirits of the world and not to Christ," (Colossians 2:8; Moffett's translation).

Other Christians scoff at the very idea of any such broad-reaching conspiracy.

"If we are going to warn, let us warn against real things, rather than against a giant theory," says Jim McKeever of Omega Ministries in Medford, Oregon, publisher of the *End-Times News Digest*. He points out that exciting tales of conspiracy and antichrist plots come and go with certain regularity.

They make good reading, he said.

They sell books.

"People love to be scared to death," he said. "This is why people pay money to go to horror movies and to ride roller coasters. There are many authors and speakers who spend a lot of time and energy creating fear among the body of Christ and the body seems to love it.

"However," he quotes, "fear is not of God, for His perfect love casts out fear" (1 John 4:18).

McKeever sees the biggest danger of the New Age movement as the division among Christians that the rash of denunciations has created. "I believe the Lord is trying to get the true soldiers of Jesus Christ to become united. Today there are many things that would tend to divide them and this is one of those. The reason for this is that once somebody gets hooked on a conspiracy theory, he begins to see it everywhere he looks. In this case, it would seem there is a 'New Ager' under every bush, just like people saw a Communist under every rock in the McCarthy era."

Another noted Christian lecturer says she became concerned at how so many Christians seemed to become obsessed with the New Age movement when she talked about it — and were filled with fear and dread.

It was as if they'd never before heard the age-old deceptions of Satan. Paul told the church in Corinth: "Satan himself masquerades as an angel of light, so it is no surprise if his ministers also masquerade as ministers of righteousness" (2 Cor. 11:14,15).

How do we fight back?

With prayer and fasting ... and discernment.

One speaker asserts that popular rainbow candles, trivets, mobiles, wind chimes and decals are signs by which secret New Agers can recognize each other — as with the secret ΙΧΘΥΣ sign of the fish in the days of the early church.

"They're signalling one to another," she says. "You'd better be careful about showing a rainbow in your window. Somebody will come up to you and think you're a like believer.

"The New Agers in America are pushing hard to instill their beliefs in the general public and especially children," she says. "They have people in high places — particularly in entertainment. How long has it been since you saw a TV show that treated Christians as normal human beings? But have you seen Saturday morning TV? Very few cartoons are not filled with the overtly occult — wizards, witches, magic, potions, crystal balls, special powers, you name it."

She goes on to say that the New Age philosophy is manifested in everyday items as the Care Bears — magic-wielding Saturday morning cartoon characters often featured on children's clothing and novelty items.

But convinced as she is that the New Age movement is everywhere — from health food stores to groups that promote breast feeding, from churches that promote prosperity teaching to the Smurfs cartoon characters — she repeats that there is a bigger danger in living in fear of the New Age movement.

"I don't like to talk about the New Age movement," she says. "We're not supposed to live in fear of Satan and that's what this so often leads to."

Indeed, if there is a plot meant to usher in the Antichrist, how are Christians to react?

By refusing to display rainbows, the symbol of God's promise to Noah? By becoming hostile and accusing toward anyone whose theology isn't identical to ours?

By making lists of fellow Christians we believe have become ensnared by suspicious philosophies?

The apostle Paul chided his young student, Timothy, saying, "God did not give us a spirit of timidity — of cowardice, of craven and cringing and fawning fear — but He has given us a spirit of power and of love and of calm and well-balanced mind and discipline and self-control," (2 Tim. 1:7 Amplified).

And John wrote in his first epistle that we have victory over such things:

"Every spirit that does not acknowledge Jesus is not

from God. This is the spirit of the Antichrist, which you have heard is coming and even now is already in the world. You ... have overcome them, because the one who is in you is greater than the one who is in the world ... God is love. There is no fear in love," (1 John 4:3,16-18).

In most large city telephone books, a New Age Center is listed in the church Yellow Pages. Steeped in the occult and the unabashed worship of Satan, the New Age movement has its roots in the Theosophical Society, founded by Mrs. Blavatsky. A basic teaching was that all religions have common truths which make up for the differences. The Unitarians and Universalists believe the same thing.

But whereas Unitarians tend to discard most beliefs in a living, loving Deity or spiritual phenomenon, New Agers believe in the guiding spirit "masters."

Why would anybody want to join such a cult?

Christian author Dennis Bennett says that such groups draw "together many who are seeking spiritual power without God, or through lesser gods, that is, spirits. Those who turn away from the true God always reach out for other gods."

New Age psychic Robert Stevens admits, "Our meditation meetings are a place that people can come to get all their questions answered — no matter what they are."

He explained that the movement believes that the "New Age" will be a time in the future in which man will have evolved into the highest level that can be obtained.

In a concept very similar to what Mormons believe, some New Agers believe that in this "New Age," men will become gods.

Isn't this exactly the lie that Satan tempted Eve with

when bringing about the fall of man? The scripture reads: "And the serpent said unto the woman, 'You shall not surely die: For God knows that in the day you eat the fruit, your eyes shall be opened, and you shall be as gods ...'" (Gen. 3:1-5).

So, indeed, is this anything new at all?

Experienced cult watchers such as the Christian Research Institute acknowledge that there is a New Age movement and that it is widespread.

"But far from being a tightly organized conspiracy," noted Randy Frame in *Christianity Today,* "the cult watchers maintain that the movement is better understood as a philosophy, a type of 'Westernized Eastern Mysticism' with elements of humanism and the occult."

The movement is immense, says the editor of a mimeographed newsletter that came to my home.

"The New Age movement is a worldwide coalition of nearly 10,000 organizations that are dedicated to bringing in a new world order to create harmony in our troubled society. The bond which unites them is their desire to promote a 'new world view' based on humanism, holistic health ideals, the human potential movement and traditional Eastern religions in order to revitalize humanity," she said in a recent issue.

"A New Age directory listed about 10,000 New Age organizations plus their branches here in the United States and Canada," according to the newsletter. "Directories have been published very openly and can be purchased over the counter in most major bookstores."

I called the editor of the newsletter and she admitted she did not have such a directory, but that she had seen one at a lecture by William M. Bowen Jr., author of *Globalism: America's Demise.*

Bowen, too, talks about the New Age threat. His book focuses more on the threat of a one-world government, the sort of warnings that the John Birch Society has been raising against the United Nations and communists for years.

"I thumbed through the directory," said the editor. "You'll be surprised at what you'll find."

Well, I looked one up at a local bookstore.

The directory is in many ways similar to the "Whole Earth Catalogue," popular in the 1970s. What's listed? Book stores, health food emporiums, holistic health massage parlors and metaphysical science communes.

"I don't know what there is to get upset about," said a spokesman for the publisher. "It's just some nice places you can visit." Indeed, it is hard to see how this rather obnoxious directory of Yoga summer camps and palm readers represents any world threatening "10,000 organizations dedicated to bringing in a new world order."

So why do Christians rise up in fear of such a thing?

They've been seduced into getting all upset about a cause other than winning souls to Christ.

They've been tricked to take their eyes off their hope and stare intently at the fear and hopelessness that the enemy waves in their face.

Like the apostle Peter, they'd rather look at the towering waves of the storm than gaze into the peaceful face of our Lord.

And like him, if they're not careful, they'll sink beneath the tumult.

The Lord grabbed Peter before he went under.

But because of his lack of faith, Peter failed to walk any more than a couple of steps on the water.

He was too accustomed to fearing instead of trusting.

Fear. Okay, you say, how do I overcome fear? The solution is simple, but not easy. You can do it the first time you try. But it's not a one-shot cure. You have to make it a part of your lifestyle.

First, you admit a very simple thing which you already know to be true: Jesus is Lord.

Second, you give everything in your life to him. Everything — including your fears. You tell Him all about them. You detail them. And you give them up to Him. You admit that without Him, you don't have any power over the things that scare the socks off of you.

Third, since the Lord says He answers our prayers, you thank Him for protecting you and answering this deep need that you've laid at His feet.

And fourth, when the fear arises again, you praise the Lord, thanking Him for His protection, delighting in His love for you, praising His greatness. Humbly, you praise Him for allowing you to be part of His great plan.

And fifth, you begin reading your Bible daily. In it, you're going to find more reasons not to fear than I can detail here.

You're going to encounter stories of when the Lord delivered His people.

You're going to find verses that you'll want to write down or even memorize. You're going to read promises that will come to you later.

And in the midst of a new fear, you're going to know that you can praise the Lord for His mighty greatness, because just this morning, you were reading the seventh verse of the 138th Psalm, in which the no-longer-fearful David wrote:

"Though I am surrounded by troubles, You will bring me safely through them. You will clench Your fist against

my angry enemies. Your power will save me."
And you will not be afraid.

12

Surrendering

Little DeWayne Jones, youngest member of the famous Gospel Singin' Jones Family, had a problem.

He was miserably unhappy.

But it was nothing he could talk about.

He kept it to himself ... except with members of his parent's country Gospel band. The band members were really his only friends. They'd turned him on to marijuana back when he was still in elementary school.

And now as a junior high schooler, he really believed he had to get stoned on drugs with the band before he could endure church appearances.

It was a big joke. Little DeWayne laughed to himself as he stared with contempt at the auditoriums full of smiling, naive Christians.

You see, the crowds loved him.

Ever since he was little, he'd stepped bravely up to the microphone and belted out "Jesus Loves Me" or "Amazing Grace" in a high, little-boy voice deep with a Nashville drawl.

Manuella and Walter Jones didn't know what to do

about their tormented, gifted little boy. He had gotten out of their control too quickly.

He recorded his first gospel record at age twelve.

He was quite a precocious twelve-year-old in other ways, too.

"I first met my wife Gladys when I was twelve years old and singing at The Grand Old Opry with my family," DeWayne remembers. "I saw her sitting in the audience and thought she was the most beautiful girl I'd ever seen."

He asked her out — to share a cherry soda after the concert. Like everything else in DeWayne Jones's life, he started early.

And no matter what he did, he wasn't happy.

Success did not equal happiness.

He'd begun his career at age four when his mom and dad stood him up on a piano bench before a stage microphone and let him join a concert of The Gospel Singin' Jones Family.

The cute toddler was an immediate hit and a natural ham, playing to the audience like a veteran. But becoming a featured attraction of a music ministry didn't make little DeWayne a believer. He lacked any relationship whatever with Jesus.

Everything was show.

As he grew older, he learned the vital need of maintaining appearances of being a good little Christian if the Gospel Singin' Jones Family's records were going to sell and if the group was going to remain in demand at concerts.

The image had to be maintained.

The lie.

And in the middle of this great falsehood, little

DeWayne Jones searched desperately for truth. Instead he found escape. Drugs. He could smile and laugh and appear at ease and at peace — and the crowds could assume it was the Lord. But in fact, unstoned, he would have put his inner torment in the spotlight. He might have denounced them or done something obscene.

Surrounded by the glitter of three-ring Christianity, he didn't look to the Lord for help. "I couldn't see through the religion to see Jesus," he remembers. His family's public faith was all flash and sequins.

"My mother was always a godly woman, but my daddy was a real hard man," he remembers. The family's music ministry was business first, an artistic outlet second, then an evangelistic outreach only incidentally.

Walter Jones "never claimed to be a Christian," DeWayne began to realize. "I never heard him read the Word at home and he never prayed with me." DeWayne never heard his father address the Lord ... except publicly — making a big, ostentatious show. With his mellow voice and imposing stage presence, Walter could work the crowd into a religious frenzy — with tears streaming down their cheeks, their hearts touched by words he was repeating from other people's sermons, testimonies and altar calls.

But backstage, he was just a businessman counting the night's receipts, negotiating the next record contract and hustling, hustling, hustling ... determined to provide the best for his family.

By the time DeWayne was in junior high, he was taking drugs regularly before he would come on stage with his family. He remained the rosy-cheeked, cute little boy who played bass guitar with the band and still did solos of "Jesus Loves Me," "Jesus Wants Me for a

Sunbeam" and "The B-I-B-L-E."

The adoring adults didn't suspect he was higher than a kite and laughing hilariously at them.

"As a kid, I was a Gospel singer who never led anybody to the Lord," Jones remembers, adding that he wouldn't have known what to tell somebody who had come to him wanting advice on how to walk closer to the Lord.

DeWayne had no such walk.

"I sang about Jesus, but I was gettin' loaded as a little guy," he recounts. "I was singing 'Amazing Grace' and taking acid at the same time."

Frequently DeWayne was so bombed during Gospel Singin' Jones Family concerts that he would become swept away by a single note on his bass guitar. Walking around the stage, he would play it over and over while the rest of the family attempted to continue singing, pretending nothing was happening.

DeWayne was desperately looking for happiness.
Happiness.

He remembers being "forced" to go to church. "I went, but I never listened," he says. Traveling and performing, the boy began writing gospel songs, but was filled with conflicts and contradictions. He didn't believe what he sang — and thus when he was rejected by other kids, was filled with anger.

Boys his age assumed the little "preacher-boy" didn't want to hear dirty jokes. But he did — if it meant being included. They figured he wouldn't want to be part of pranks or troublemaking. But he most desperately did.

Happiness...*happiness.*

Frantically little DeWayne cast about searching for **happiness.**

Instead, he was stung by the alienation and social

rejection that is suffered by young Christians. But —
lacking any relationship with the Lord, he had no refuge.

Unlike a Christian kid who has a relationship with
the Lord, young DeWayne was spiritually exiled, trapped
by a false "religious image" he had to maintain, but
believing not one shred of the Christianity that he
flaunted since his family's image required it.

In his loneliness and unhappiness, he turned to
songwriting. And he was good.

At age seventeen, a song he wrote was recorded by one
of the superstars of country music. DeWayne became
wealthy virtually overnight. In the first year, he made
$90,000 in royalties.

"After the first album was such a hit, 126 albums by
other people were released with that song on them," he
remembers. Big groups and well-known artists began
recording DeWayne Jones compositions.

They had no idea there was nothing behind the religious façade of the talented boy from the respected
Gospel Singin' Jones Family.

Young Jones had learned how to fake Christianity in
his songwriting just as easily as he could fake it in his
public performances.

And suddenly rich, he left the family singing group
and — in a frenzy, he tore after happiness.

He was rich.

He was young.

He was talented.

And now he was wealthy.

He could have anything.

Even happiness.

He became a close friend of ex-Beatle George Harrison,
by then a movie producer and Hare Khrisna Hindu-sect

disciple. He got stoned with the bitterly unhappy Elvis Presley.

"Me and Elvis used to get high together," he remembers. "We lived in castles together."

Castles.

"When Elvis died, he choked to death on his own vomit," Jones remembers. "Now that's not pretty, but it's true." He hesitates. "Let me tell you — castles are lonely."

Unhappy castles of fame and success and riches.

Where is happiness to be found?

How do you find it?

Can you buy it somewhere?

Can you achieve it out of sheer determination?

This is a question many people — the DeWayne Joneses and George Harrisons and Elvis Presleys and you and I — have each asked, usually just in private, but often in near desperation.

Lord, why can't I be happy?

As DeWayne Jones discovered, it won't work without a key component, a vital missing ingredient.

Surrender. Write this down and put it on your bathroom mirror: The secret to happiness is *surrender*.

This goes far beyond a one-time shot of inviting Jesus into your heart or a public profession of your Christian faith. ***Surrender.***

It's not part-two of conversion. It's not something new and controversial, a second experience, an add-on step to holiness or a work by which you can become worthy.

In theory, surrender ought to come when we become a Christian. But unfortunately, it takes years for some to discover our need for surrender.

Surrender.

Resting in the peace of Jesus.

Accepting the mercy of our Lord.

Relaxing in His plan.

Waiting on God.

Listening to His still, small voice in our heart.

Surrender.

Dying to ourselves. Taking on a servant's heart.

At age twenty-two, Jones ran into his future wife, Gladys, again.

"At first I didn't recognize her," he remembers. "She was all grown up, a woman. But I fell in love with her all over again."

They got married.

She had gone through a brief rebellion, but was now a devoted, surrendered Christian.

But DeWayne was uninterested in turning anything in his life over to the Lord.

So Gladys began several very difficult years of praying for her wild husband. His drugs and antics continued. His pictures showed up in fan magazines, wild-eyed and crazy-looking with the greats of rock music — with whom he was writing music, playing his guitar and partying for days on end in Europe, in the Orient, in New York, in Los Angeles.

He could be seen everywhere: His name was on record jackets and concert credits with his friends — Little Richard, Billy Joel, Eric Clapton, Willie Nelson, The Who, The Rolling Stones, Harrison and scores of others.

He became addicted to heroin and constantly experimented with a variety of other drugs. He fell into a downward spiral seen too often in the entertainment world. He would spend every dollar he and his wife owned, then cut a new record, go on an extended concert tour, make thousands of dollars, spend every cent on drugs, parties, other women, excitement and more drugs. Then, his money gone, he would record another album and go back on tour.

Then on such a downspin in 1974 he overdosed on heroin. His heart stopped briefly in the emergency room. He was revived, but it had been too close, he and Gladys both knew. He began going to church with her, but was not satisfied.

"I found a Bible study where they ignored me. I would go even if I was stoned. I was trying to seek the Lord, but I wasn't really sold out."

After the fellowship groups, DeWayne would drop off his wife, then go meet friends to discuss the Bible and snort cocaine. His double life went on for years as the battle for his soul raged inside.

He could try to be a Christian, but he could not surrender.

He could not give up everything.

"I must've gone to the altar a hundred times over the years," he says.

Then in 1979, Walter Jones lay terminally ill in a Nashville cancer ward.

"One day, I went to the hospital to see my daddy and he started telling me about Jesus," remembers Jones. "Now, I loved my daddy, but I never liked him. We never got along. We hadn't spoken to each other in a long time. I was going to the hospital because he was dying and I felt guilty.

"But that last year before he died, he started reading the Word of God, and God really broke his heart. The Lordship of Jesus Christ became real in his life. When I saw this hard, cold man that I never wanted to be around become a sincere, kind, gentle person, then I began to visit him because I wanted to, not out of guilt.

"I told him I loved him and if I'd known our relationship could have been like this, I wouldn't have spent all these years fussing and fighting with him."

DeWayne was unprepared for his father's reaction. Walter Jones was a big man, six-feet-five-inches and 280 pounds. DeWayne had never seen him cry. But he cried that night. He told DeWayne, "Son, Jesus has really come into my life and really touched my heart."

Deep in DeWayne's heart, a years-old longing was met. A chord was struck and the son answered the father with tears of his own.

DeWayne went home that night and asked the Lord to do a miracle in his life like the one He had done in his father's.

And this time, DeWayne began to see the need to surrender everything.

"Nobody knew when I became a Christian because I didn't tell anybody at first," he says. At a loss as to where to seek fellowship, he remembered his family's old home church in Nashville.

He slipped quietly into a service. But he was recognized by old-timers and staff. He was welcomed home like a prodigal son.

"The most astounding thing about DeWayne was the effect the Word of God had on him," former youth pastor Jim Smith remembers. "For a long time, he came to Bible studies and then the Word began to take root in his heart. As it did, it began to heal his mind. By the time he finally stood up to sing to the kids at church, he was truly anointed by God."

But still Jones could not surrender all parts of his life.

He dabbled in the drugs that had been a vital part of his life ever since before his teen years.

After all, it was part of his lifestyle, he felt.

Surely the Lord doesn't expect you to remake your whole personality.

"I remember one time he shared that he had taken drugs over the weekend," remembers Smith. "We were shocked, but the honesty with which he shared his struggle completely took us aback."

The last time Jones took drugs was in 1980, he says. He tried to witness to a rock star friend, who instead got him to get high for "old times."

"I tried to tell him about the Lord, but I was in the flesh," says Jones. "I was so guilty and frustrated afterwards and the Lord told me, 'Look, you don't have to go through this again.' What He showed me was I simply needed to draw close to Him."

The healing of Jones's mind after decades of drug abuse amazed Smith. But another healing is more amazing to Jones: the healing of his marriage.

"Jesus forgave me and that's miraculous," he says, "but sometimes I feel Gladys' forgiving me and loving me is even more miraculous. What God has done in my marriage, I can't tell you in words."

As DeWayne's faith increased and as his personal discipline developed, Evangel Temple's confidence in him grew. The music that had so long been a part of his life finally meant something to him.

Now he sang about a Lord with whom he had a deep and personal relationship.

He began a youth outreach with a band of Christian friends formerly in secular rock. Today they have a very successful Christian music ministry.

Jones says he is determined not to let his growing popularity turn into the money-centered type of Christian business that he grew up in.

"We don't advertise and we never have had an agency to book concerts," he says. "We just answer the phone at church and if people invite us to come and minister, we pray about it. We never say, 'Okay, we'll come if you give us 'x' amount of dollars.'

"My purpose for going out on the road is not T-shirt and record sales. I was already selling millions of records. My purpose is those people in our prayer room after a concert—the ones who came down at the altar call. My life no longer belongs to me. The One who's running my life is doing an incredible job. I couldn't buy that with $20 million."

He's determined not to let his popularity get in the way of his personal witness, either. Jones believes fervently in the need for Christians to witness one-to-one on a daily basis and to live lives that shine a light of hope to a searching world.

He's surrendered.

There's a new move of the Lord in young people like DeWayne who have seen the prostitution of the gospel and are willing to go sing and preach without pay.

They don't go in their own power. They are supernatural warriors. And their ministry is going to take them through the fire. Like Astrid and Tom and Leisha and little Amelia and the kids at Island Pond, they've seen and known the protection of God.

Like David and Daniel and Jehoshaphat, they have seen the shallowness of the Satan's lies — the glittery sham of his empty pleasures. And, instead, they have chosen God's goodness.

And His might.

And His power.

Such strong spiritual warriors will make up our new generation of evangelistic leaders.

God is going to humble the spiritual gurus enmeshed in their time-wasting religious political games.

He's going to turn His face from the power-brokers trying to set their own place at the table at the right hand of God.

He's going to throw into real poverty those defiling the gospel by only trying to make a buck off of Jesus Christ.

That's all coming down.

New warriors are rising up.

With pure hearts.

The Lord is revealing himself to the ones honestly seeking Him — and less to the ones out there prostituting His Kingdom.

He's going to empower the warriors in the trenches ... not the pretenders hiding in ivory towers.

How? How will He bring down the deceivers?

The frauds only think they know how to fight back — but in reality they have fallen prey to their false god, Lucifer.

Thank God that righteousness will prevail and God will vindicate His saints.

The righteous live by faith and have a blessed hope. We are clothed in His righteousness and Christ has many, many rewards prepared for us. Some are even given to us here on earth.

In the Book of Revelation we read, "...his bride has made herself ready. Fine linen was given to her to wear. Fine linen stands for the righteous acts of the saints" (Rev. 19:7-8).

Thank God that righteousness will prevail and God will vindicate His saints.

13

A Brush
with Death

At a freeway off-ramp in Colorado Springs, the little station wagon was making a left turn. The light turned, the driver took her foot off the brake and stepped on the accelerator.

Just like hundreds of times before, she entered the intersection.

But this time, her world suddenly collapsed in a grinding crash of metal and a shower of exploding glass. Everything went black as a fuel truck slammed into the little car, spun its shattered frame around and pushed the twisted hulk toward the power lines. The station wagon's driver slumped over the wheel, unconscious.

In the terrible silence, witnesses gasped at the horrible sight.

"Dear God!" whispered somebody.

"Is she dead?"

"Somebody get help—**please!**"

Running to the wreck, a young man tried to wrench

open the station wagon's door. But there was the strong
smell of oil and gasoline. He knew he had to get her out
before the fuel truck and twisted car erupted into flames
— or else the woman would be burned alive!

But she remained slumped, motionless over the
wheel—her face a mass of blood and glass.

Reacting quickly, the young man yelled at a bystander
to help him rip away the sun roof. As the two peered
down at the woman, they realized she was having
difficulty breathing. The young men reached into the car
and held up her head cautiously.

I had been on the way to my office to sign some letters
before catching a flight to a two-day speaking engagement. I was getting ready for a trip to Holland, where I
intended to confront a large group of satanists that had
contacted me. Worship of the devil is particularly blatant
in the Netherlands—the seemingly peaceful land of
windmills, tulips, dikes and Hans Brinker. At the driver's
wheel, my ministry's executive director, John Arana,
suddenly slowed. "Nicky, that looks like a bad, ugly
accident, " he said.

I nodded. "It looks pretty bad."

As we neared, I peered at the crumpled little car.
Then, the stunning reality hit me.

I screamed, "Dear Jesus, that's my car! Gloria, Gloria.
Jesus that is my precious wife Gloria! My best friend! My
only real confidante on Earth!" For a fleeting moment, I
dared not believe that she was still alive.

"Please, God," I prayed, "don't let her suffer."

John saw, too. He stopped the car with a screeching
halt.

But I was already out of the car and running to the
wreck before it stopped. The young man on the roof

asked who I was as I gently reached in to touch my beloved.

"That's my wife. That's my wife!" I shouted in anguish. I took her head in my hands and began to think and pray. Suddenly everything within me, my emotions, my sense of time, my awareness of what was going on around us, seemed to be frozen in time and space. I just could not believe that my wife was sitting there, hopeless—blood oozing from her face, her mouth, her hands. My heart cried out within me as I beseeched the Lord to preserve her life.

Just minutes before she had pulled out of our family driveway to take our daughter, Elena, to school.

"Good-bye," Gloria had said as she gave me a kiss, "I'll see you in two days. Have a good crusade."

Now she lay crushed, pinned in the twisted metal, unconscious—dying for all I knew. Deep feelings of pain and sorrow such as I'd never felt before swept through me. This was the one woman that I loved. The mother of my children. My best friend. My love. My moral support. My emotional stability in times of trouble. Broken. Bloody. In great pain. Then I began to hear a moaning. She was trying to assure me that she was okay. But she could not talk. She was in terrible pain but still trying to comfort me, reassure me that everything would be all right. She hurt. But my Gloria was trying to be strong.

Wasn't that just like her? Trying to help me when it was she who was in agony. In a whisper, I prayed over her. And I could tell that she could recognize my voice. My heart leaped within me for joy and my faith went into action.

I had seen blood before.

Many times.

As a street kid, I had held my best friend, Manny, in my arms as he clutched onto life. It had been snowing. The sky was grey. I was on my knees, hugging Manny to my chest, rocking back and forth in despair, knowing the ambulance would not arrive in time. As the blood from his thirty-two switchblade stab wounds soaked the ground about us, he breathed a deep sigh—then no more. I had been filled with intense anger. I would avenge him. I would kill those who had killed him.

I screamed aloud to the cold, grey sky, "Why God? Why have You allowed Manny to die? Even if You exist You ain't no friend of mine. I am certainly no longer interested in You. Let's face it God, I have never believed in You anyhow." Kneeling in the bloody snow, I had nowhere to turn. I was at an emotional, psychological, physical and spiritual dead end.

But this wasn't Manny. This was my beloved Gloria. And I was no longer that restless young lion, the rebel without a cause, searching the skies for answers or solutions. Now I had the Lord Jesus Christ with me.

As I held her head gently and watched her pain, I wanted so much to embrace her and convey to her my love and support. But I couldn't. I had to hold her head steady in my hands. I had to protect her neck.

Otherwise, she might be paralyzed. How I wanted to scream but my system was totally shut down.

In the midst of this rush of emotion, I hoped and prayed that there was no danger of that. I could see that her leg had been shattered. There was no way I could move her since the metal pinned her to the seat. At that moment, I realized how much different this situation was from Manny's death. Now, I was not in defiance of God. This time, He was my friend. The Creator of the universe—the only One who could keep Gloria safe and alive until help arrived.

The smell of gasoline seemed to be every where and was burning my nostrils. Would we make it? I couldn't help but wonder if we would in an instant meet Jesus together in a blazing inferno? However, the peace of God was everywhere. I remained quiet and calm.

Gloria knew Jesus, too. Unlike Manny, she was filled with faith. A faith strengthened by hours of prayer and years of trusting dependence on Him.

Again, I whispered a prayer and had an unusual sense of the Holy Spirit's presence. I glanced around and saw John torn apart in tears crying out to God in prayer. That stunned me. As desperate and confused as I was by the accident, I was not afraid. I had a strange sense of God's power flooding the inside of the twisted little car. Somehow I knew she would live.

So powerful was it that I felt that the Lord was holding Gloria to His chest—since I couldn't. He was taking her pain upon Himself, as I would have done if I could. As I trembled, I felt the literal presence of Jesus Christ. He was there. In the wrecked car beside us. I bowed myself to His authority. I thanked Him. I praised Him. I worshiped Him.

As I held my hands steady to protect her head, I knew Jesus was comforting her, speaking to her unconscious mind, reassuring her gentle spirit.

Tenderly and compassionately, He spoke to my heart: "Take care of the natural. Don't worry. I will handle the supernatural."

I looked up.

I saw the fury of the holy, mighty army of God. Angels of the Lord were engaged in battle against the forces of death and destruction. I rejoiced. There was no way the angel of death could get near our twisted station wagon, for it was surrounded by great supernatural beings. And as I gazed out at this mighty display, I heard the still small voice of the Lord. "Gloria belongs to Me. She is My daughter. She is dedicated to Me. I will protect her."

I knew God was moving heaven and earth for this one dear woman. My spirit began to rejoice at the victory I was witnessing. "Thank you, Jesus," I murmured. I felt like a little child thanking my Daddy for the greatest gift He had ever given to me.

In that moment, Gloria regained consciousness. Although she was bleeding heavily and had bones broken, she understood I was there. As she slipped back out of awareness, I sensed her complete trust in the Lord. I was filled with a tremendous feeling of relief and gratitude.

One of the most beautiful things to see was the sincere concern of the people around me. A woman came forward and gave me one of her business cards. She had been a witness to the accident, and said that the truck had been at fault. She told me that she was willing to do anything to help us.

My heart pounded as I heard the screams and wails of the ambulance sirens. "Hurry, please hurry. Please Jesus, get them here and fast," I prayed. Suddenly the ambulance and emergency vehicles were there. Almost instantly workers were moving the truck.

As our little station wagon shook and dropped to the ground, I felt the pain rip through Gloria. Yet, I also felt the presence of God all over the car. I knew that Gloria was surrounded by an invisible power force protecting her and watching over her as the twisted metal was removed that imprisoned her.

The paramedics began to move her gently. Quickly they placed a brace on her neck, then very carefully put her on a stretcher. I had so many questions. I needed comfort.

As I raised my eyes and looked at the paramedics and the gathering crowd, I felt so helpless. I was painfully searching for hope, for an answer. For the first time, I was so insufficient and insecure. My whole world was crushed and I was transported to the Twilight Zone of true reality. Where once I shared her joy, I now was feeling her pain.

"How is she going to be? Where are you taking her? Is she dying? How much pain is she having?" I quickly asked.

Although the paramedic's answer was vague, I sensed a deep kindness and concern for me. I think he truly understood how I felt. I was at peace. God had empowered me in a supernatural way. He had given me a glimpse of His power and His army.

Like lightning they put Gloria into the ambulance. "Oh, Jesus," I cried, "now I know somewhat how your mother Mary felt as she stood and watched You suffer on the Cross."

The trip to the hospital seemed to take forever, even though it was only a few moments before we were there. "Jesus, please release Your miracle working power over Gloria," I pleaded.

Indeed, she did experience a number of miracles— including a medically inexplicable halt in the internal bleeding while she was in the Emergency Room.

As I paced back and forth praying, suddenly I heard, "Mr. Cruz, your wife has suffered a great amount of trauma, a great deal of blood loss and a near fatal accident. She also has bones broken in five different places. I personally don't understand all that is going on but I believe your wife Gloria will be all right. She will be in the Intensive Care Unit for some time. Why don't you leave for awhile and come back in several hours. Perhaps then you can talk to your wife."

I thanked the doctor and decided to go to my office and make some phone calls to tell friends and family about the accident.

When I stepped inside of my office every fiber in my body seemed to come unglued. I wept, screamed, prayed and cried. There were moments of thanksgiving for the miracles that had already happened and then suddenly there were also moments of wonder and fear.

"Jesus, please I beg You, be in total control. Please Jesus, for I know that I am not in control of myself or the situation right now. I have lost it!" I cried. Suddenly like the softness and gentleness of a Spring rain, I felt the presence of the Holy Spirit engulfing me. Then I was at peace and again I knew everything would be fine.

I began to understand the restlessness I had been feeling for two weeks. I had felt it as I delivered a message at an outreach conference. I had felt it when Gloria and I talked about a book I wanted to write — a spiritual warfare manual for believers.

"Are you going to write about witchcraft again?" she had asked.

"No," I had assured her. "In this book, I want to warn of the forces that corrupt the Church and Christians."

But I had understood her concern. While I was writing *Devil on the Run,* all hell had broken loose—literally. We had faced all types of demonic attack.

I told Gloria I was firmly committed to exposing the

devices of the enemy. She had nodded silently. "Nicky," she had said, "I'm beginning to see you go through some changes. We cannot allow our family to go through what we went through last time."

"I understand," I had assured her. But I had been torn apart. In the next weeks, she and I would travel to England where we would see twelve straight days of power and glory as young people packed auditoriums and gave their lives to Jesus. From there, without any rest, I would go to Poland.

There, one of the most magnificent things was to see Gloria's face light up with joy and love as thousands of people responded to the message. In Warsaw, 2,500 came to the Lord in one night.

They had seen the movie, *The Cross and the Switchblade*—in which actor Erik Estrada plays me and Pat Boone plays David Wilkerson. Polish versions of my book, *Run, Baby, Run,* had been widely distributed before the crusades.

So, the people pressed forward, wanting to meet me, to shake my hand, to have me pray with them.

Several times, we'd almost been crushed by the people pressing close. Gloria had been scared. Security guards escorted us out to safety, past clutching, reaching people with tears of joy on their faces. I was so moved during that tour of Poland. I sensed a great move of God's Spirit. For the first time, we were permitted to pass out literature and to put counseling material in the hands of those who streamed forward to the altar. It was a spiritual explosion. We saw 6,300 come to Jesus in those few days.

"Gloria," I had said, "This is the place for you and I. These people are virgins in their hearts—they are not corrupted. They are not materialistic or hedonistic. They don't want to hear prosperity nor legalism. They are hungry and thirsty for God alone."

Gloria nodded in awe. Together, we pledged that upon our next visit, we would gain permission to bring in 75,000 Bibles.

Over the next months, that became my goal, dream, prayer and desire. It turned into an intense passion, a drive compelling and consuming me. Yet, at the same time, we were having increasing confrontations with satanists in Holland. In recent months they'd become particularly bold—disrupting my crusades and flaunting their evil-glorifying worship of Lucifer.

Satan is misunderstood, they teach in dark sanctuaries filled with up to 500 members with absolutely no moral values. God isn't as good nor mighty as the Bible says—according to these angry, self-gratification-obsessed people, whose services are filled with sex, animal sacrifice, and unholy sacraments such as a profane anti-communion served before a reclining, nude woman.

Such seems impossible in America.

Yet, it is growing. I believe it is just one more sign that the end of time is upon us. These confused, power-hungry people are readying for the return of their great, evil messiah—the Antichrist.

The irony is so incredibly heart-breaking. I encountered them in Holland—a free, capitalistic, democratic, member of the western alliance and NATO—a country that evokes thoughts of windmills, tulips, wooden shoes and wholesome children ice-skating on picturesque canals. It's the land of Hans Brinker, Corrie ten Boom and good Queen Juliana. But in the company of Dutch Satanists, one feels as if one has returned to Noah's day or Sodom and Gomorrah.

Yet, among the yearning Christians of Poland, I felt as if I were walking through the book of Acts. These people were committed to the death—standing up for Christ in a dark, communistic land filled with fear and death. They were experiencing God's mighty power. It had been wonderful for me to experience their joy with my beautiful Gloria at my side.

Gloria....

When I arrived back at the hospital, she urged me to catch a plane and go ahead to my scheduled two-day speaking engagement. "Go for it!" she enthused from her bed in the Intensive Care Unit. "Go on! Conquer!"

"Honey you have got to be kidding. I love God with all my heart, but leave you alone? Never! I will cancel the meetings, " I firmly said.

"Nicky, in my heart I know that you must go—you must go! I know it is God's will for you to go and serve Him and leave me in His hands, " she said with quiet spiritual authority.

"Gloria, honey, are you sure that God wants me to go?" I asked in bewilderment.

"Yes, Nicky, you must go," she responded.

With tears running down my cheeks I said, "Honey, thank you for being such a wonderful woman of God. I have no other choice but to go." I gently kissed her and left the room ready to bawl my eyes out with both joy and sadness.

All the way to the Colorado Springs Airport I thought my heart would break. But I also knew I had to go ... it was God's will.

As I arrived at the Denver airport, I went to wait for my connecting flight.

"Nicky, Nicky Cruz," I heard my name being called. I

looked up and there stood a minister that recognized me.

"Nicky, I am so burdened for you." He then took my hand and began to pray, "Lord Jesus ..." and away he went, praying for the Lord to encourage Gloria and me, to protect us, lift our spirits and to give us God's peace. What an encouragement his prayer was — my heart leaped in thanksgiving.

I suspect that we may have looked like a couple of fools right there in the middle of the waiting area, but that man just joyfully raised his heart to heaven.

I don't even know his name. He said the Lord had guided him to be there to meet me and pray for me.

He had not heard anything about Gloria's accident yet. But as I told him a little of what had happened, I secretly thanked God for having someone waiting there with a message of hope. It had been no coincidence.

Then, on the plane, the evil darkness made one last attempt. I found myself sitting next to a professing witch—which, as you know, has happened before.

But this time, I was filled with greater boldness.

"You can't touch me," I spoke to the evil one within her. "I belong to Jesus."

The woman sneered.

But she left me alone in my thoughts.

Six days after the accident, Gloria was released from the hospital. Today she remembers little of the wreck, except that I was there with her—somehow. But she is quick to give the praise and glory to Jesus. He delivered her from what appeared to be certain death.

By the time she had arrived at the hospital, there was no sign of any glass cuts on her face, although it was covered with blood. Jesus had taken her pain and her fear.

There was little that remained as evidence of her escape from death. But I was there. And I remember.

I remember the presence of the Lord—and how He always comes through.

I remember the angels.

I remember the peace.

And I remember the victory.

14

Jamie Buckingham's Close Encounter

Author Jamie Buckingham and I began our close friendship when he was a struggling preacher at a little congregation meeting in a day-care center in Eau Gallie, Florida.

I was a poorly educated, jitterbugging New York street kid, astonished that the story of my conversion had been turned into a bestselling book and popular movie, The *Cross and the Switchblade*.

Over the years, Jamie and I were to go through a lot of things together — not the least the traumatic collapse of Logos International publishers, *Logos Journal* and the *National Courier* newspaper. We both lost a lot of hard-earned money there, believing in a dream that was not to be.

If you have read Jamie's books *Risky Living, A Way Through the Wilderness, Daughter of Destiny, My Summer of Miracles* or his monthly column in *Charisma* magazine, you undoubtedly chuckled at his candid appraisals of God's moves in everyday life.

One night back when I was struggling through Bible college, Jamie and I sat down at a kitchen table and he helped me begin to write down my testimony. It became the bestselling book *Run Baby Run*.

That cooperative effort was both his and my first book.

We've both gone on to write quite a few others. He's written maybe 40, such as the remarkable *Power for Living* and several with such notable people as Kathryn Kuhlman, the Happy Goodman Family, Congressman/ Astronaut Bill Nelson and Corrie ten Boom.

So, it was quite a shock when a friend of mine from his church recently stuck a postscript on a fax message to my office: "Did you know Jamie Buckingham has cancer and isn't expected to live?"

In shock, I called up Jamie. It was true. The doctor basically had told him to go home and die.

On *The 700 Club,* Pat Robertson would announce to the world that Jamie had been diagnosed with terminal cancer — inoperable, incurable ... fatal. Pat would challenge all Christians to intercede for Jamie.

But that afternoon, I prayed with Jamie and was touched by his lack of fear. His spirits were good. He was fighting — hard. He began to share with me, his voice perhaps a little shaky.

Across the globe, thousands of Christians were praying for him — and he felt their prayers. That was an incredible experience, he said.

"It's been the finest week of my life," he said. "It's been the most glorious week in my life. The scariest week of my life.

"The thing that has happened between me and God is indescribable."

As I talked with him, it all seemed too unreal. Jamie with cancer was impossible. A few years ago, depressed by his approaching fiftieth birthday, Jamie had been feeling the physical and psychological impacts of middle-age — and the reality that he would not be young forever.

Jamie had told me that he felt God promise him that he would live another 50 years ... if Jamie would cooperate with Him. He thought this meant he had to take care of himself, lose weight and begin to exercise. I had to agree strongly with him. The Lord had shown me that I would feel better and live longer if I, too, would keep my body healthy.

As a result, I became a runner. I love speeding on foot down a deserted beach, around a quiet park or through a beautiful forest. It is a joy surpassed by few other things in the physical realm of God's creation.

Jamie took up basketball, racquetball, running — you name it. But was that what God really meant when He told Jamie to cooperate with Him?

"I was wrong, Nicky," Jamie confessed on the phone. "I tried to do it all in my own strength. What God meant was that I had to let Him be God. I had to quit trying to do it myself.

"So one day on the racquetball court, I played for about five minutes, and suddenly I went into total exhaustion," Jamie told me. "I couldn't catch my breath. All the energy had left my body.

"I'd never had a feeling like this, Nicky. It was the weirdest feeling I've ever had in all of my life. I got off the court and told the guys I was playing with, 'I gotta go get a drink of water.' But I couldn't have swallowed anything.

"I just wanted to get away from them. I was embarrassed over what was happening to me. I wandered around, trying to breathe. I finally went back and played, but I didn't play very hard. I was glad to finish the game."

That night, he ran a slight fever. So, the next day, he went to a doctor, who examined him, took a lot of blood and a week later had grim suspicions: "The blood test shows a possibility of lymphoma." Cancer of the lymph system. A CAT scan showed ominous shadows on one of his kidneys, too.

From the pulpit, Jamie shared the bad news with his congregation, the Tabernacle Church of Melbourne, Florida, which long ago grew out of the Eau Gallie day-care center to fill up a half-block.

The people of the congregation began fervent prayer — including a daily 6 a.m. men's prayer service, attended by as many as 300 men.

But the news grew worse.

"We're diagnosing it definitely as renal cell carcinoma of the left kidney, which essentially is inoperable," the doctor told Jamie. "It won't do any good to do any surgery."

Jamie was diagnosed as being in the final stages of terminal cancer. The doctor just shook his head at the idea of chemotherapy or radiation. The cancer was too far along, already up into the lymph glands, bones, and spreading throughout Jamie's chest.

Jamie was going to die, said the doctor. No treatment was recommended.

Did Jamie go into a panic?

No.

When I called, he was at peace.

He was not surrendering.

He was fighting back — in new and wonderful ways. Mostly, he was learning how to trust in the Lord.

"Nicky, I've determined that the confession of my mouth is going to be God," he said.

The goodness of God.

His mercy.

His providence.

His healing.

His sovereignty.

"At the hospital they asked me to fill out a form when I came in for the bone scan the other day. 'Have you ever, do you have cancer?' it asked.

"I didn't fill it in. I put a little note down at the bottom that said, 'The doctors say I do.' That was kind of silly. I'm not going to put my head in the sand, and try to act like a Christian Scientist and say the cancer is not there.

"It is there, Nicky. I know when I'm standing that my back is tired and hurts just a little bit. But everything else seems normal. My energy level's a little low. If I run up the steps I can tell it."

My eyes filled with moisture. I knew my friend was aching with a deep hurt of body and, yes, spirit. There had to be resentment there, back in the bottom of his heart, crying out to God: "Why? Why? Why?"

"Nicky, I don't know where we're going from here," he told me. "I have no idea what this holds. I've cancelled out everything on my schedule. I just don't know what's going to happen."

Then he got deadly serious. We shared an honesty that I remembered from those naive, innocent days when we worked on *Run Baby Run* together.

"I've spent most of my adult ministry repeating and filtering what everybody else is saying," Jamie quietly confessed. "And people have said, 'Boy, Jamie knows more about what's going on in the Kingdom than anybody else.' Well, Nicky, I didn't know anything. I just knew what everybody else was saying. You don't know anything about the Kingdom until you know the King."

I chuckled with him. But I sensed how serious he was. It can be such a temptation when you or I are so good with words that we can easily preach a dynamic sermon that will break people's hearts. We can move folks to do anything we want ... yet, our powerful, human words can be so stale and empty and nothing but theatrics.

I knew what he was saying.

I have been there.

"A lot of the things that I have been preaching, I haven't known anything about," he told me. "I haven't known anything about facing death. I've never faced death in all my life. I thought I had another fifty years. I'm fifty-eight and I'm really proud of the fact that I can keep up with most of the guys that are twenty years younger than I am.

"But this week everything has changed. We turned the TV set off. There's been no need to watch anything. When you focus in on God, it really doesn't make any difference what's happening any place else. We laid down the newspaper.

"I've been the busiest guy in the world. I've not had time for my wife, I've not had time for my family. I've not had time for God. I can preach without praying. I can get good ideas. I don't have to hear from God for a lot of things."

I knew what he was saying. Without the Lord empowering you, as you attempt to preach without God's strength, without His might, without His timing and without His power, many preachers can belt out a pretty good sermon.

And the preacher who does it feels so empty afterwards. So ashamed. You stand up there and act like you heard something from God, but you are only recycling old stuff — from earlier anointings and other people's wisdom.

And you want to fall on your face in shame.

When you can finally get alone with the Lord, you pray that you will never again be so presumptuous, so prideful, so unable to look out at the people and say "I'm not prepared tonight to change anybody's lives because I missed an appointment with my Father to seek Him and find out what He wanted me to say tonight."

It takes guts to lean into the microphone and shamefacedly ask the congregation to pray with you that you will not sin by pretending to speak in God's strength when you are preaching in your own cleverness and knowledge alone.

It's scary.

They may titter and giggle and lose respect for you — as you deserve.

Or they may, as I know has happened with my old mentor David Wilkerson, fall on their faces before the Lord with you. They may humbly and honestly and joyously seek Him and ask Him to speak to them tonight.

I know one time when Dave fell before the Lord for maybe 40 minutes, just moaning and crying out in emptiness and human weakness, asking God to show him His way, His truth, His life.

When Dave got up, he didn't expect anybody to still be there. But no, everybody was there with him, tears running down their cheeks, their hearts torn in two. And it wasn't because David Wilkerson had put on some dramatics.

It was because they, too, had been seeking their great and wonderful God. And they had been asking Him to speak.

And He did. And His greatness and majesty had never before been more present.

Quietly, I listened to Jamie's wry voice.

And I chose to believe with him that he was going to be healed. That he was already healed.

That this was not "unto death."

But that was not the end of the battle.

15

Don't Fight Alone

"We haven't been able to find a Christian doctor, and I'm talking to secular physicians who don't understand where I'm coming from, which makes it much more difficult," Jamie Buckingham told me days after his terminal cancer was diagnosed.

When he talked about prayer and healing or the massive intercession going on worldwide on his behalf, the doctors would bob their heads respectfully, but they didn't take it seriously.

Why didn't Jamie already have a Christian doctor? Well, I've had the same problem. If you are blessed with excellent health for decades, you don't need a doctor.

Jamie hadn't even gone in for a checkup in years. He hadn't ever been a patient in a hospital. He wasn't even born in a hospital.

I understood his frustration. As I knelt in the twisted metal of my wife's car, as I felt the presence of angels, as I felt God's glorious assurance that she was going to be okay, I also knew that the paramedics did not.

At the hospital, the doctors and nurses just didn't understand that our situation was so different from the other patients who didn't know Jesus.

Many were Christians — and attended church. But they still didn't understand.

They didn't grasp that we believed in and trusted a great God who is sovereign over incurable diseases or irreversible injuries.

Jamie told me how Bernie May, the president of Wycliffe Bible Translators, called. They had put word of his diagnosis out on their computer network, all over the globe. Wycliffe is the largest missionary organization in the world.

"So last week, when all these Bible translators worldwide cranked up their computers," Jamie chuckled, "there was a prayer request that came upon the screen to pray for Jamie and Jackie Buckingham.

"The request was very odd, too. Wycliffe asked them to pray a Scripture verse for us. 'God will keep them in perfect peace, whose mind is stayed on him.'

"Naturally, Nicky, I thought, 'No, pray for my healing.' Then I realized, 'No, they have the right prayer.' I need God's perfect peace.

"I talked to Oral Roberts on the phone the other night. He called me, crying, weeping and saying, 'I have faith to believe for you, that this is not your time to go. But the Spirit of God will have to give you that same faith. My faith is not enough. He'll have to give it to you.'

"We talked for a long time and he said, 'Now, I want to pray for you. But before I do, you've got to pray for me. You know, I had tuberculosis as a young fellow and almost died. Thought I was dead. God's healed me from that. But my lungs are still weak, and still scarred, and I've got a horrible cough.' I could hear him coughing, coughing, coughing.

"Oral said, 'Nobody knows I'm sick. Nobody's praying for me. Word's gone out that you're sick, and a lot of folks are praying for you. But nobody's praying for me. Would you pray for me?'

"Suddenly I was consumed with a spirit of intercession. I've not been praying for people. I get prayer letters from missionaries, I just kind of glance at them and throw them in the trash can because I'm so busy. I stood the other night in the kitchen, for twenty minutes, praying for somebody from China — just because their prayer letter had come.

"Now Jackie and I frequently pray in bed at night, early in the morning, before we get up — as well as other times, such as when we're in the car. We pray more for others than we pray for ourselves. We've been overwhelmed with the need to pray for one another and with the powerful need for Christians to pray for one another. We've got to stop judging each other and stop criticizing each other. We must pray for one another.

"So I prayed for Oral. And he prayed for me, and he said, 'You know, as you pray for others, healing comes to you.' I think that's why I'm in this situation. I had been moving in my own strength, doing my own thing and not listening to the Lord."

As I prayed with Jamie, I've got to tell you, I had to wrestle with a sincere concern. Life is so hard sometimes. Our burdens, our disappointments are just so tough. And the Father has such a marvelous reward waiting for us in heaven.

For all eternity, we will just rest in His goodness,

enveloped in His love, singing His praises and adoration.

How could I pray that my friend Jamie not get his reward? How could I pray that Jamie have to stick it out down here, fighting the devil, battling cancer and enduring the human weaknesses of our human bodies?

I didn't share that doubt. Instead, Jamie confessed to me how he found himself going from such highs to such lows. He had no difficulty believing God would heal him. But his mind would raise new doubts, worries and concerns.

"I start thinking about what the doctors have said — and none of it is good," he said, his voice grim. "It's my nature to pick up books, and to rush through them and find out what my odds are. I'm not going to do that. Somebody else can. I am going to listen to God. "

Days later, Jamie again encountered resistance from his doctors when he insisted that they operate to remove the cancer.

They said the malignancy was too far along.

They said there was no point in treating it — that it would just come back.

Jamie had better put his affairs in order, they calmly advised him.

He was a dead man.

But my friend had heard the Lord.

He was supposed to go ahead with the surgery.

Have you ever heard the voice of the Lord? For most of us, it comes as a still, gentle assurance deep within.

Marcus, one of my co-workers, once fell to his knees in agony after hearing that a dear friend named Sarah had been killed in a freak auto accident.

"No, dear Lord," prayed my friend, "let it be somebody else. Let it be a mistake."

Then, deep within him, Marcus knew that it had not been a mistake. Sarah had strayed from the Lord for years, but in recent months had returned and gotten her life together.

She was a weak Christian.

She was not strong in the Lord.

She was prone to wavering.

But today she was ready to meet her Maker. And it was a kind and loving God who would take her now.

Although Marcus did not hear a thunderous voice from heaven, he knew there had been no mistake.

And he felt immense shame for doubting the wisdom and timing of the Lord. Why pray that it had been some stranger who might not have known Jesus?

"Forgive me, Father," Marcus wept, his face wet, pressed against the floor. "Thank you for Your goodness. Thank you for your mercy to Sarah."

The Bible tells of Moses talking with God.

Of the apostle Peter hearing God's clear voice.

Today, hearing the Lord's voice is a marvelous thing. When it happens to you, you will know.

Even so, seek the Word. Does what you heard agree with the Bible? Seek counsel from discerning, solid Christians. Don't, for example, announce the day that Jesus is returning or go start a new denomination just because you heard a voice.

The devil can deceive us.

When someone else claims that God told them to tell you to do something, weigh it carefully against the Word before you act. Go to the Lord in fervent prayer. Does this "word" given to you agree with what the Spirit of the Lord tells you deep in your spirit?

Again, seek counsel from discerning, solid Christians

— particularly Bible-studying elders in your fellowship, people who have been given places of authority in your church.

Why?

I know people who actually commit the blasphemy of claiming to hear from the Lord when they want to win an argument.

You say yes, they say no. You insist on yes, they stand firm on no. You begin to offer irrefutable evidence that the answer is yes. Then, they announce that the Lord Almighty told them no — and declare loudly that if you are going to persist in this rebellion, then you are fighting the very powers of heaven in your human deception.

Whew! How do you argue against that?

Remember, just because somebody makes a good argument does not make them right.

Just because they can brow-beat you or out-shout you does not give them wisdom.

Losing an argument does not make you wrong.

Sometimes, you just have to quietly hold onto that which you know is true — particularly if you are falsely accused and lack the verbal skills to let anybody see the error of your loud, bullying accusers.

Seek the Lord's wisdom.

Ask Him for the right words.

He will give them to you.

Remember this vital, important truth: You cannot win against the forces of deception in your own strength.

You and I cannot out-shout Satan.

But the Lord can silence his lies and empower you with just the right word — the effective rebuttal that will silence the banshee howls.

Or a mighty demonstration of His power.

Jamie Buckingham heard from the Lord that he was healed — and that he was supposed to go ahead with the surgery that the doctors said was pointless. Over and over, Jamie heard the Lord assuring him that he would be healed if he would just cooperate with Him.

His doctors smiled benignly, patiently, patronizingly as he insisted on the surgery. They glanced at the X-rays and CAT scans and biopsy reports that said Jamie was a dead man.

They frowned and winced when he insisted that they operate. They told him that this sort of cancer spreads like wildfire when the patient is opened up — that it was better if he would just accept his fate and go home and die.

They were tired of arguing about it with a medical layman, this wide-eyed preacher with a pie-in-the-sky, mystical, marvelous fantasy that some Deity was going to intervene against a cancer that was beyond healing.

"God spoke to me, almost audibly," Jamie told me, "just as I was waking every morning, Monday through Friday. He spoke to me. And it was on a Thursday morning of that week when He said, 'Cooperate with me, and I will heal you.'

"I grabbed onto the word 'heal,' because I wanted to hear it so badly. And I said, 'Lord, I will.'

"And He healed me."

Was it as simple as that? Across the globe, friends and strangers were interceding. In the offices of Christian nutritionist Dr. Mary Ruth Swope, an employee named Julie Frahm had a special burden for Jamie.

Here is what she felt the Lord telling her:

"This sickness is not unto death," she told friends at a

Thursday night home fellowship. "But Satan wants Jamie to die. As I was praying this morning, I felt that the faithful prayers of thousands of intercessors have had a very real effect.

"It is as if the constant petition against this thing has pushed Satan back a mile ... but that we still have a couple of yards to go. And we cannot give up just because this thing is almost over."

Jamie, too, felt the prayers.

And these were not ordinary prayers for mere healing. In the 6 a.m. men's meetings at his Tabernacle Church, the prayer was often on anything but Jamie. On their faces before the Lord, the men of "the Tab" heard God's will for cleaning up their own acts — making things right in their households, restoring relationships and changing the way they were living.

"Oh, Lord, forgive us," wept one man at the altar. "We have looked to Jamie Buckingham and not to You. We have put him on a pedestal and listened to him — and not sought Your voice ourselves."

Like a chorus, the other 300 men joined with him, beseeching the Lord to forgive their idolatry — their putting their pastor before Jesus.

"Forgive us, Lord, do not take him from us for this sin," cried out another man. "Create in us new hearts, yearning for Your presence and Your righteousness. Let us keep our eyes on You, not Jamie."

Across the platform of the Tabernacle Church, men stumbled and wept and bowed before their God, tearfully repenting of their sin — and of their own failures to live in God's strength or to fight back in His power alone.

Some felt another conviction. Why weren't they praying like this for everyone in the church — on a regular basis? Why had it taken the near-death of their pastor to drive them to their knees?

Surely the rest of the congregation was just as deserving of such intercession — the third-grader battling leukemia, the Air Force master sergeant facing forced retirement because of a recurring brain tumor, and the old lady battling cancer of the spleen.

And so, the prayers were lifted up for these little, seemingly insignificant ones. Of course, the men continued to intercede for the pastor that they so loved.

And as they and the whole world prayed, Jamie felt the certainty that he was to have surgery. Couldn't the Lord heal Jamie without his going under the knife?

Isn't God more powerful than any doctor?

Oh, yes.

But God heals in wondrous, mysterious ways.

In 2 Kings 5, the Lord could have healed the pagan warrior Naaman instantly. Instead, He told him to go out of his way, travel to the river Jordan and humiliate himself publicly by dipping himself repeatedly in the water.

And Paul didn't touch Timothy and give him instant healing — or order the young preacher to fall to his knees in search of healing in 1 Timothy 5:23, but instead told him to quit drinking the polluted water — and to have a bit of medicinal wine for his frequent stomach problems.

The prophet Isaiah didn't lay hands on Hezekiah in 2 Kings 20:7, but instead, gave him a divinely ordered prescription. Read it for yourself!

Jesus healed a blind man by dabbing mud over his eyes in John 9 and ordering him to wash it off in the Pool of Siloam. Then in Mark 9, Jesus spit on his hands, then laid them on another blind man — who had to receive the

Lord's touch a second time before he could see clearly.

So, it is wrong to think God only heals instantly.

It is a mistake to order God around, too.

It is not faith when you decide that He will heal in some way that you have decided it ought to be done.

Faith is when we believe without physical proof that God has done what He says He will do — particularly when we cannot see any results ... yet!

The doctors in Melbourne refused to do the surgery. Jamie had to fly to Houston, Texas, before he found physicians who agreed to try.

On the operating table, Jamie's kidney was removed. Samples of his lymph system and bone were removed for testing.

As he was recovering in his hospital bed, the pathology reports began coming in.

Apparently there had been a mistake.

His lymph system was not cancerous.

There was no cancer in his bones.

Nothing had spread up into his chest, as had been feared. Yes, the kidney was diseased.

But the cancer was basically confined there.

And all of it had been removed on the operating table.

All of it.

In his subsequent book, *My Summer of Miracles*, Jamie proclaimed his complete healing. Joyously, victoriously, he declared the great thing that God has done.

As I talked with Jamie, here was the magnificent part: *My dear friend Jamie did not fear death.* Not at all.

He just didn't want to go before his time!

So, how are you and I to fight back when a good friend comes under this kind of assault — particularly a recurring illness such as this?

Close friends lived through that terrible trauma when David Wilkerson's beloved wife Gwen fought battle after battle with cancer — a story I detailed in my book *David Wilkerson: A Final Warning*.

How did God allow it? How did He permit such a godly and wonderful woman as Gwen to be hit over and over with cancer? To have to undergo repeated therapy and surgery?

Why?

Why did God allow Jamie, so delighted with his healing, to have a relapse on Good Friday — a new, different type of tumor in his spinal column that would require diligent radiation therapy?

Why? Why when our Lord could banish the sickness from Gwen's or Jamie's bodies?

Why?

So many times I have heard Jamie talk of dear friends whom God chose not to miraculously heal. Why did great Christian figures Kathryn Kuhlman, David de Plessis and Catherine Marshall die like they did?

Why did the Lord let Corrie ten Boom, whose testimony was told so mightily in the acclaimed bestselling book and movie *The Hiding Place,* suffer for so many years before He took her home?

Why did the Father allow bold athlete and missionary Eric Liddell of the Oscar-winning *Chariots of Fire* to suffer and die like he did in China?

Here is the answer proclaimed by Jamie time after time:

"Let God be God."

Proclaim His goodness.

Thank Him in your time of trouble.

Rejoice when things look absolutely black.

Because He is there.

He does not bring us out into the wilderness for no good reason.

He is God.

And He knows what He is doing.

That does not mean that I should not continue fighting back for any good friend of mine who is battling against untimely death or inexplicable illness.

Nor should I feel defeat when someone is ushered home to their reward.

God will not turn His back on our pleas.

Nor will He betray us.

It is our place to rejoice — and know that He is God.

Satan would love to silence our proclamations of victory. What a defeat if the forces of hell could twist our view of God's goodness and parade defeat before the people of God when a godly friend is ushered into eternal joy.

Should we not pray?

Should we not earnestly intercede?

Yes, we must! There are so many times in the Bible when the Lord heard the prayers of His people and changed the course of history.

And there are other times when He did not.

Jesus perspired drops of blood as He fervently prayed that the Father not require Him to go through the looming betrayal, trial and crucifixion.

"Take this cup from me," He requested from His Father as He knelt there in the Garden of Gethsemane.

But our Father did not grant that plea. He had a bigger picture spread before Him of the salvation of all of mankind.

Jesus, instead, died.

Of course, He rose again. And praise God that our great Creator stuck to His mighty plan instead of responding to the heartfelt plea of His beloved Son.

Jesus submitted to the will of the Father, resting in the truth that God knew what He was doing.

Jesus submitted.

As must you and I.

It is not always easy.

Keep that one that you love on your prayer list.

Believe that he or she is healed. Amen! They are completely healed. Let us agree together that he or she is going to stay healthy and that Satan will have no victory from this incident.

And let us stay submissive to our mighty Lord, to rejoice and to be glad if the Father chooses not to alter the course of His magnificent plan.

In our prayers, we can cite His promises in His Word to heal, restore and deliver. In our hearts, we can hold tight to His mighty assurances — building within our spirits an ever increasing faith.

But if we are to effectively fight back, we soldiers in the trenches cannot order around the Supreme Commander.

Even if He does things we do not understand.

16

Never Quit Fighting Back

Word reached me that there were militant satanists in the crusade crowd. Someone had sent up a note to the platform, letting me know they were there.

Some of these people are downright unpleasant.

They're so aggressive in their hatred of Jesus Christ that they will burst into a meeting, chanting, accusing, demanding equal time and denouncing the speaker in blunt obscenities.

Some of them you may know by name from the news media. Several are such publicity hounds that I'd rather not give them any more recognition here in my book.

That night, I knew they didn't really want to debate. They were not trying to establish truth through an exchange of ideas.

Perhaps, they would just try to wear me down — insulting me, making wild accusations against the people on the platform, and generally disrupting things until chaos reigned.

This was not a night that I wanted to engage in hand-to-hand spiritual combat. I was exhausted.

After an exhilarating series of crusades in England, I had been delayed at London's Gatwick Airport as my international flight connections changed unexpectedly. That had really frustrated me, because I needed to get to my next engagement early so I could rest and recharge my spiritual batteries.

Now I would only have one day before I was to speak in Vancouver at a youth crusade drawing 1,500 kids.

Then my flight was delayed in Montreal, causing me to miss my flight out of St. Louis. So, instead of a day off, I hung around airports for eighteen hours and got home to Colorado Springs at midnight.

At 6 a.m. I flew to the crusade on the West Coast.

Jet-lagged beyond belief.

Exhausted physically.

Washed out emotionally.

Just before the song service, I was passed a note. The Satanists wanted me to know that they were not going to rush the stage and take over the microphone — instead, they said they were conjuring up a great, evil spell, summoning the evil powers of darkness to confuse and confound me and to destroy the crusade.

Oh, great.

Just what I needed.

"We're praying that all the forces of evil will destroy you, kill you and throw down everything that you have worked for," it said.

With no time to prepare, I went silently before the Lord. I asked for His power, His strength, His boldness, His timing ... and His joyous, merciful inspiration — giving me the right thing to say.

They wanted a supernatural confrontation. They wanted to demonstrate publicly that the gospel had no power to change lives. They wanted to seduce the thousands of kids in our audience with a demonstration of their exciting power.

I saw that they were not there only to entice teens, but to check me out — the ex-leader of a big street gang and the son of a satanic high priest.

And the Lord opened my eyes to something downright spooky. These kooks weren't really out for a confrontation within natural dimensions. No, they were fighting us in the heavenlies, in the supernatural realm — praying to their dark lord, beseeching the evil spirits of the air to confuse and destroy us.

"Ah, Nicky," you may sigh, "Come on, this sounds like the Twilight Zone."

My friends, this sort of thing is very real in these latter days. Did you know that shortly before Jim Bakker and Jimmy Swaggart fell into their individual scandals, that modern witches marched around and around the national headquarters of the Assemblies of God?

This story is recorded by bestselling author Dr. David Allen Lewis, who wrote *Prophecy 2000* and *Smashing the Gates of Hell*.

From midnight until 2 a.m., the witches did a Jericho march around the Assemblies headquarters in Springfield, Missouri, praying to their evil master to humiliate top leaders of the denomination through immorality.

Both Swaggart and Bakker had Assemblies credentials. Soon afterwards, they suffered horrible national scandals in which both had to confess humiliating sex sin.

No, the evil power is real.

But we are not defeated!

As I stepped into the pulpit, I spotted the trouble-makers. They looked like something out of *The Rocky Horror Picture Show* — complete with safety pins in their ears, black lipstick, lacy brassieres and corsets over their black T-shirts and Lycra pants.

Here is what is remarkable. They had been at the two previous nights of the crusade. Thursday and Friday had been powerful and anointed, despite my personal exhaustion.

Every night, these bizarre folks had been seated up front, to my right. But when Saturday came around, I knew that someone had to make a move because the services had been too strong and convicting.

During those evenings, and now as I preached in the power of the Holy Spirit this Saturday night, the young people faced up to their hang-ups, weaknesses and corruption by sex, violence, rebellion, witchcraft and drugs. That night, there was a fantastic altar call.

It was then that the satanists made their move. The leader sent another note to me on the platform as the aisle filled with kids repenting of their sins.

This new note proclaimed that Satan was stronger than Jesus Christ, that Christ had no power, and that this group of satanists was there to curse the service.

It said that they were there to embarrass me and shame me. They said Satan was in control of the earth and that Christ had no control over Satan's domain.

Then, the note sneered, there would be a spiritual war that night and Satan would win. As I read this garbage, the power of the Lord came over me, filling me with a Spirit-given boldness and firmness.

"You!" I proclaimed, pointing at them from the pulpit.

"You there! I know who you are. I know what you are! Make your move! You will not have the victory. I rebuke you in Jesus' Name.

"Don't mess around with me! Let's get it together, man! Come on, attack! It's your move, man! Go for it, here I am! Come on!"

I scared that punk leader, frightening him to his core.

"Greater is He that is in me than the evil one that is in you!" I shouted — pointing right at him. "No evil that possesses you can touch me or any other person in this crusade tonight. We are here to claim victory! You demons in him, leave these people alone! The only place for you to go is back to hell!"

I like to think that all my time as a kid in the street gangs of New York City was not entirely wasted.

I learned how to street brawl.

And I know that the best defense is always a strong pre-emptive attack before your enemy is ready to jump you.

Believe me when I say that this is how we must fight Satan. Boldly. Unafraid. With bare knuckles.

This satanist leader, a young man of about twenty years, began shaking. The Lord revealed to me what kind of guy this young opponent was — and very quickly I realized that he was just a scared kid deceived into fighting in the wrong army.

He was a confused, troubled, battered boy looking for answers.

I was filled with mercy as this young soldier in Satan's evil army was filled with genuine conviction and repentance. Running to the altar, the boy cried out and confessed his sin, asking God to help him.

He had been molested by his father and therefore had

no respect for any authority. He had started hanging out with satanists at fourteen years of age. He looked rough.

Praise God, that night, he repented.

I put my arm around him and prayed for him.

"Nicky," he said. "They will try to kill me. You can't turn your back on the satanists. Pray that I will be strong. I know now that Jesus Christ is the answer and that God alone is the one true Master of the universe and that only He is in control!"

He cried.

His heart was broken by the power of the Holy Spirit.

I sent him home with some strong Christians who cared for him and nurtured him in his new walk with Jesus. He had, indeed, been severely abused as a child. He had terrible hurts that only Jesus Christ can heal.

He came to my crusade ready to riot and burn.

But instead, he checked into the Holy Ghost Hospital.

Today, he serves Jesus Christ.

My friend, you are equipped to fight back.

You are destined to win!

No satanist can silence you!

No modern-day witch can destroy you!

No godless welfare department can take your kids! With God on your side, no wacko anti-God militant is going to disrupt your revival!

And no sin can separate you from the love of your Father. Sure, you may have to pay the earthly consequences.

But we win every time — you and me ... and Jesus.

At the National Religious Broadcasters annual convention in Washington, D.C., Christian humorist Mike Warnke was scheduled to debate a modern-day warlock, live on national radio on the Bob Larson talk show.

But instead of a knock-down, drag-out, this male witch began telling why he knew that Christianity was fake — detailing the disappointments he had suffered as a child inflicted with parent-mandated Sunday school.

Gently, Warnke backed off from the debate and agreed with the warlock that Christians are seldom perfect — and that the ones the warlock was describing had genuinely blown it.

Before the end of the hour, the warlock had accepted Jesus as his personal Savior.

Hallelujah!

Can God do the impossible?

What a silly question, Nicky, you may chuckle.

But it's the key to fighting back.

Nothing is impossible for God.

And He loves us so much.

He's ready to march into battle for us.

He will send in His angels, too, to assist us! In the Book of Daniel, we read how the Lord allowed the prayer warrior Daniel to glimpse some of the warfare that goes on over us in the heavenlies. God showed Daniel that he had responded to his prayers. As a result, the great archangel Michael was locked in battle with the demonic "Prince of Persia" for many days!

I believe that evil entity is still lurking over the defiled land now called Iran! Remember the terrible confusion that American forces suffered when Jimmy Carter was president and he attempted to send in commandos to rescue our hostages in the American embassy?

For no apparent reason, our crack troops were confounded and confused. In a surprise sandstorm, American aircraft began colliding with one another in a terrible loss of life.

Why? Because evil forces were arrayed in the heavenlies! And they were unopposed!

Our God is the One you want on your side when you undertake such spiritual battle. What a difference we saw in the Desert Storm war of 1991 when millions of Americans were on their knees, praying for the safe return of our forces.

What victory resulted — at such a small loss to our armies!

God triumphs over such evil every time — if He is invited. In response to our prayers, He will send angelic forces such as the Archangel Michael, who I believe has been given great authority in heaven and on earth to destroy or to protect cities and nations. Michael is my personal hero. He is the mighty warrior who battled Satan for Moses' body and who led the triumphant campaign against the demonic rebellion in heaven eons ago.

Gabriel is the messenger in the Gospels, the great archangel who gave the virgin, Mary, the incredible news that she was to give birth to the Son of God. Gabriel is the messenger of God, the one who brought the good news of Christ's birth to the shepherds. He is the angel with a strong sense of peace, just as Christ is the Prince of Peace.

Lucifer, however, is the archangel who had the sensitive position of being the leader of all of the worship in the heavenlies. Lucifer is a tragic figure who deserves no pity. He, apparently, was a favorite of the Lord — was the heavenly choir director, the leader of praise and worship at the very throne of God.

But he led a rebellion.

He foolishly tried to overthrow the Creator of all

things, the Master of all that is — the mighty One who allows you and me to call him Father.

Now, banished from the joyous presence of the only true power in the universe, Lucifer is called many names — Beelzebub, the Lord of the Flies, the Father of Lies, the Old Serpent, Belial, Prince of Darkness, the Great Red Dragon, the Tempter, the god of this world, and Satan.

But God turned His face from that rebel so long ago. Nothing that Satan does can prosper against us! In fact, our struggle with him is leading up to the greatest *StarWars* in the history of the world.

This spiritual battle in the heavenlies is in preparation for the Second Coming of our Lord Jesus Christ.

Satan has so many weapons against us.

Do not be deceived! He is the author of cleverness and cunning. To the person who consumes alcohol, he comes as the finest liquor available. To the person that lusts, he comes as the most voluptuous woman or the most handsome Adonis.

And to the person who does not know the Word of God, he comes as a religious spirit posing as the Holy Spirit.

How he rages against God.

How he hates all that symbolizes his terrible loss! How he desires to spoil that which God loves — to hurt our Father by deceiving, seducing and enslaving His children.

But he only wields lies. Here's a letter that I received recently at my office from an inmate serving a fifty-year sentence in the Arkansas Department of Correction for murder.

It's a good example of "postal evangelism" — winning people Jesus using something like the mail. You see, evangelism is one of our most powerful weapons against Satan. And I hope this shows that you don't have to be a crusade evangelist to win the lost!

You just have to care. Because the man knew of my reputation with the gangs, he had contacted me through the mail. He wrote that he thought I was the only one who could understand his predicament.

I wrote him several times, witnessing to him and taking authority over Satan. It was not just Nicky Cruz, but the combined efforts of the Nicky Cruz Outreach staff and people with a prison ministry personally talking with him that brought him peace and deliverance through Christ.

At age eleven, according to the letter, he was introduced to satanism.

"During my first initiation, I was put upon an altar and sexually assaulted in every manner possible by the older, male members of the coven. Though in pain, it was okay as long as I didn't lose the acceptance and approval of my new friends."

"Although I was only a sixth grader, I started drinking and using every drug I could get my hands on. My family believed my problems were due to my extreme hyperactivity. I was sent to a child psychiatrist and placed on medication. Though the medication helped calm me down some, it did nothing to slow down my gang activities or my worship of Satan.

"In 1975, at the age of twelve, I moved to the Philippines with my family. There I became more deeply immersed in the occultic world and participated in numerous rituals in the jungles outside of the base. I was taught the use of animal sacrifices and how to summon demons to cast a hex or spell.

"We returned to the states in 1977. By all outward appearances, I was a normal, fourteen-year-old boy. But inside, I was a satanist, alcoholic, drug addict, and barely in control of normal functions. I experienced periods of deep depression and would fly into blind rages. I stole constantly from my own family. My mind was littered with the abuse of drugs, alcohol, illicit sex, lies and the delusions of those who serve Satan.

"At fifteen, I decided to run away from home. After stealing a pistol, I took off. A twenty-two-year-old college student offered me a ride.

"As we neared the ramp where the young man was to leave the freeway. I pulled the pistol from my waistband and placed it to his head. As he complied with my demands, a voice in my head began to scream, 'Kill him! Kill him!'

"I tried to force the idea from my mind, but it persisted. Over the next ten minutes it became almost a chant inside my mind. I felt terrified and yet the chant, the voice screaming in my head persisted until I finally decided that the young man would die.

"The college student begged me not to shoot him and I assured him I would not. We smoked a marijuana joint together.

"I then told him to walk into the woods and informed him I was taking his car.

"As he turned back around, the voice in my head screamed, 'Kill him!' I instantly raised the gun and pulled the trigger, shooting him in the head. As he fell, I continued pulling the trigger until the gun was empty.

"As I looked down, dazed and shocked at what I had done, I screamed at him to get up. I ran back to the car and tore back to the highway, my mind racing while in the back of the car, I heard laughter.

"I took the pistol and put it to my own head, hesitated and pulled the trigger. I threw the gun to the floor of the car cursing. It was out of bullets.

"I was arrested two days later still driving the young man's car. I tried to outrun the officers chasing me, trying to force them to shoot me. I was forced off the road, arrested, and eventually sent back to the state where the murder took place. I was tried as an adult, and sentenced to fifty years in the Arkansas Department of Correction.

"In 1979, I entered the prison with the notoriety of being the youngest inmate in the facility.

"My first night was spent being raped in an open-man dorm in front of eighty men," he recalls. "A man without Christ is subject to the environment he lives in. I was no exception. Over the next several years, I was to go through never-ending cycles of depression, rage, and rebellion. My bitterness grew in the belly of a corrupt system and as I aged, I became what I was subjected to; no longer a receiver of aggression as on that first night, but an aggressor in the jungle I called home."

But now, he has come to the Lord.

"In August of 1990, after twelve and a half years of confinement, I was on one of my numerous trips to the 'hole' for violating an institutional rule. I smuggled a razor blade to my cell with full intentions of taking my life. All of the anger, bitterness, pain, fear and loneliness would disappear with a few strokes of a small piece of steel.

"For the first time since I could remember, I became terrified at the thought of death. Questions began to form in my mind. What if all I had chosen to believe was wrong? What if the Bible really was true, and I was going to a hell different from the one I believed to exist?

"I threw the razor against the wall, disgusted with myself and my confusion. I started reading one of the several news articles that had been printed about my life that year. On the back of one article was the address to a church in Little Rock, Arkansas. I responded. That began a process that continues today.

"I had been taught that God would not forgive me for the rituals and desecration I had participated in. That by my allegiance to Satan, I was beyond forgiveness. I had to know if that was true: Would God forgive me for all of the filth, all of the times I had persecuted His followers and cursed His Name? Would God reach as low as I was?

"The forces of my evil lord tried to stop what was happening. It was as if the demons of hell were scrambling back and forth screaming, 'He's searching! He's questioning! Send in Doubt, Discouragement, and Anger!'

"On November 28, 1990 at 2:30 a.m. I was tossing in bed trying to make sense of all I'd read that day. The weight of my life became too much to bear and I broke.

"Tears streamed down my face and with them came the first of many earnest prayers to a powerful, forgiving and loving God. Most of all, a forgiving God. It was like lancing a large, festering boil and the pressure behind it was tremendous. All of the bitterness, confusion and fear shot out and I was powerless to stop it, such was its force.

"Some of the convicts who had known me for years thought I was losing my mind, but I was finding the healing power of the Savior, Jesus Christ.

"I literally pounded at the doors of heaven, screaming to be let in.

"I thank God and praise Him that He was right there to cleanse and heal my battered soul! I knew right then that Almighty God heard my prayer, that He loved me and His angels were rejoicing in heaven because I had found the Savior of the world!

"That morning as I watched the sun rise through the bar-covered windows, I felt a peace and comfort that was totally alien to me.

"The bars of my physical prison did not disappear that night, but the bands on my soul were broken and cast away.

"I almost wish I could say things became perfect in my life after that beautiful night of meeting Jesus Christ. I say I 'almost wish' because if it had become perfect, I would never learn to fully trust and lean on the Almighty God.

"I would never learn to listen for His voice or follow His guidance. I would still rely on just myself instead of realizing that I am nothing without Jesus Christ.

"Things did not magically change," he writes. "I still encountered the everyday problems of living in prison. Yet, everything became easier, knowing I was never alone and could overcome any problem in front of me.

"I was forgiven, cleansed and healed.

"My life was filled with knowing and hope.

"I know that my past is forgiven and cast behind Him, that I am loved and cared for.

"I have hope for a beautiful 'today,' and that in this day I will learn more of Him and serve Him more fully."

Amen!

If there's one thing that I want you to take with you after reading this book, it is that we cannot fight in our own power.

No human authority, no man could have changed this young inmate's life.

But Jesus did — as mere men fought for this kid's soul in the power and might of our great God.

And Jesus won.

You can fight back, too, my friend.

Fight in the Lord's power. To be effective you'll have to begin seeking Him anew and the Holy Spirit's power.

You've got to know His voice.

You've got to recognize His gentle guidance — as well as His divine shove.

Otherwise, you are going to get frustrated in the seeming silence and begin moving again in your own power.

How do you obey God?

How do you fight in His strength?

Go back to the Bible. Embed God's Word in your heart that you might not sin against Him — read Psalm 119:11.

It was Jesus that set this man free and gave him life.

And so it will be with you.

You can, indeed, fight back and win.

Not because of Tom and Leisha.

Or a darling little fighter named Amelia.

Nor because of Nicky Cruz.

The day of the superstar, the big name, the preacher in the spotlight is ending.

Instead, my friends, we are going to see a grassroots move of the Holy Spirit in the hearts of the little guy. That's how millions came to know the Lord behind the Iron and Bamboo Curtains during the terrible days of religious repression in Russia, China and Eastern Europe.

Those believers had to contend with false prophets, too, wolves in sheep's clothing paid by the government to serve as false teachers of a dead, powerless gospel.

But the little guy fought back.

And won.

Changing the world is up to you and me, working one-on-one with hurting people who need the real answers that come only from a God who cares.

So, stop looking for the next superstar.

It's you, caring about the hurting one God sends to you. It's you and me ... millions of us changing lives one at a time, winning the millions that the superstars simply can't reach.

You can fight back.

You can win because of the strength and power in your life that will come as you humble yourself before the great, loving God who loves you so.

He's so interested in you!

He wants you to know Him as a friend.

He wants you to be able to fight back.

Gloriously!

Victoriously!

Oh, yes, He'll help you fight back. We are to march forward with the confidence and authority given us in Christ Jesus!

Satan was defeated at the Cross of Calvary. He knows it, but my friend, we must know it — and believe it, also, as we fight back!

If you'd like to know more about Nicky Cruz Outreach or would just like to make comments, feel free to write to:

Nicky Cruz Outreach,
P.O. Box 25070, Colorado Springs, CO 80936